VIKING SOCIETY FOR NORTHERN RESEARCH
TEXT SERIES

GENERAL EDITORS

Alison Finlay and Carl Phelpstead

VOLUME XX

HRAFNAGALDUR ÓÐINS (FORSPJALLSLJÓÐ)

HRAFNAGALDUR ÓÐINS
(FORSPJALLSLJÓÐ)

EDITED WITH INTRODUCTION, NOTES AND TRANSLATION

BY

ANNETTE LASSEN

VIKING SOCIETY FOR NORTHERN RESEARCH
UNIVERSITY COLLEGE LONDON
2011

© ANNETTE LASSEN 2011

Reprinted 2012

ISBN: 978-0-903521-81-9

The illustration on the cover is from f. 80r of Melsteðs Edda, SÁM 66, Stofnun Árna Magnússonar í íslenskum fræðum, Reykjavík, a paper manuscript written in 1765–1766. Photograph by Jóhanna Ólafsdóttir. The inscriptions (normalised) read:
Heimdallur með gjallarhornið.
Þá hann blæs í hornið, heyrist um allan heim.
Heimdallur er sama og Mercurius í þeirri latínsku Eddu, hann er sendiboði guðanna og því hefur hann vængi á höfði og fótum.
Um hann má lesa XXV. eddudæmisögu.
(Heimdallr with the Gjallarhorn. When he blows on the horn, it can be heard all over the world. Heimdallr is the same as Mercury in the Latin Edda, he is a messenger of the gods and so he has wings on his head and his feet. You can read about him in Dæmisaga 25 of the Edda.)
This refers to *Laufás Edda* or to the edition of P. J. Resen, Copenhagen 1665.

Printed by Short Run Press Limited, Exeter

CONTENTS

PREFACE 6
INTRODUCTION 7
   Previous Editions 8
   DATE AND HISTORICAL CONTEXT 9
      Date 9
      Nótt skal nema nýræða til 18
      The Title *Hrafnagaldur Óðins/Forspjallsljóð* 21
      Content and Style 23
   MANUSCRIPT TRANSMISSION 26
      Description of the Manuscripts in Group A 28
      Description of the Manuscripts in Group B 35
      Description of C 64
      Description of D 65
      Description of E 67
      Relationship of the Principal Manuscripts 70
      Manuscripts Derived from Printed Books 71
      Other Manuscripts 76
      Lost Manuscripts 76
      Significance of the Manuscript Transmission for the
          Reception of Eddic Poems 78
   TREATMENT OF THE TEXT 81
TEXT AND TRANSLATION 82
COMMENTARY 95
BIBLIOGRAPHICAL REFERENCES 107
INDEX OF MANUSCRIPTS 113
INDEX OF NAMES 115

PREFACE

In the first volume of the Arnamagnæan edition of the Edda (1787), where *Hrafnagaldur Óðins* was first printed, Guðmundur Magnússon tells an anecdote about what was probably the very first study of this poem. The learned Icelandic poet Eiríkur Hallson at Höfði had spent a whole decade of the latter half of the seventeenth century on a careful examination of *Hrafnagaldur*. After ten years of desperately trying to make sense of it, he is said to have thrown his work away, saying that he still understood little or nothing of it (*abjecisse eam perhibetur, addens, nihildum se aut parum ex ista intelligere*). Since 2003, when I began researching this poem, I have often been tempted to do the same, and never during my work have I felt as nonchalant towards the not inconsiderable difficulties it presents as Finnur Magnússon, who in 1821 bragged that he had spent much less time on it than Eiríkur (*det samme... neppe har kostet mig et Par Dages Tid i det hele*) and yet had easily made sense of the poem, using his great insight into the system of Nordic mythology. But then Finnur, as one may surmise from his involvement in the notorious Runamo scandal, also had an uncanny ability to read much out of little.

If I have not despaired, this is not least thanks to the interest and help of friends and colleagues (though it goes without saying that any remaining errors are entirely my own fault). It was during a three month's stay in Reykjavík in 2003 as a fellow at Stofnun Árna Magnússonar that I began this study. Much work was also carried out in the manuscript collection of the National and University Library of Iceland and at the Centre for Manuscripts and Books at the Royal Library in Copenhagen, in which two libraries most of the manuscripts containing *Hrafnagaldur* are today to be found. I am grateful for the help I have received from the staff of these institutions, especially to Sjöfn Kristjánsdóttir and Ólöf Benediktsdóttir, who made much Icelandic material available to me while I was far away from Iceland. In the early phases of my work on this edition, the late Stefán Karlsson, with his usual generosity and helpfulness, read and commented on some of my drafts, for which I owe him much gratitude. Guðvarður Már Gunnlaugsson, Eysteinn Björnsson, Alex Speed Kjeldsen, Maria Arvidsson and Katrín Axelsdóttir also deserve my thanks for their assistance, while Einar Gunnar Pétursson discovered several additional manuscripts that until then had not been known to contain the poem. Einar Gunnar also generously shared with me his vast knowledge of the seventeenth century, for which I am grateful. While I was carrying out my work on *Hrafnagaldur*, Giovanni Verri was for a time working on his own study of six of the manuscripts of *Hrafnagaldur* found in Iceland in connection with his 2007 Bachelor's thesis at the University of Iceland, which offered the two of us a welcome oportunity to share information. I am also grateful to Christopher Sanders for his interest, practical suggestions and great stemmatological stamina. Peter Springborg, who to begin with was editor of the *Opuscula* volume in which my edition, before it grew beyond a mere article, was originally intended to be published, deserves my appreciation for much help and useful criticism. It almost goes without saying that I owe very special thanks to Anthony Faulkes, who not only generously offered to translate the whole edition from my Danish into his English, but during that work has provided detailed and useful comments, to the point of even suggesting new solutions to unsolved problems. Finally, I am sincerely grateful to Gottskálk Jensson for not losing faith in the importance of this work when I could sense a creeping doubt in myself. Thanks for your time, critical inspiration and encouragement.

Copenhagen, October 2010   Annette Lassen

INTRODUCTION

Hrafnagaldur Óðins (Forspjallsljóð) is quite a short poem (208 lines) in the eddic style, in *fornyrðislag*, which is not transmitted in medieval manuscripts. This poem, which describes an unsuccessful journey to seek wisdom, is in style and content different from the medieval eddic poems. After the description of an apparently ominous dream, Óðinn sends Heimdallur, Loki and Bragi off to find Iðunn to enquire of her about the future, but she can give no reply and weeps, apparently losing all bodily strength. Loki and Heimdallur return to the gods, who are sitting at a merry drinking feast with Óðinn and the other gods, with neither answer nor solution, and the poem concludes with the gods retiring for the night. It ends with the day breaking and Heimdallur blowing his horn.

Hrafnagaldur is first and foremost transmitted in manuscripts that contain collections of eddic poems and poems in eddic metres and go under the name of *Sæmundar Edda*, but also in a very few manuscripts of more varied content. The present investigation demonstrates that *Hrafnagaldur* is a postmedieval poem that was probably composed in connection with the enormous interest in collections of eddic poems that arose immediately after the rediscovery of the Codex Regius of the Elder Edda in 1643 and continued for some two centuries. That *Hrafnagaldur* cannot be much earlier than this is shown by among other things its use of the originally Greek proverb 'nótt skal nema nýræða til', the spread of which in Western Europe is closely bound up with the Renaissance. *Hrafnagaldur* is transmitted in at least 37 manuscripts, of which the earliest are from the second half of the seventeenth century, the latest from 1870. The present edition gives an account of the poem's transmission in the known manuscripts. The majority of these manuscripts have no text-critical value, but they nevertheless provide an insight into an obscure part of the postmedieval history of eddic poetry and bear witness to a considerable antiquarian interest in and production of manuscripts in the seventeenth, eighteenth and nineteenth centuries, primarily in Iceland, but also in Denmark and Sweden. The collection and production of manuscripts in Iceland was principally carried out by priests and other learned men.

Hrafnagaldur is transmitted in a single version, and there are only minor differences between the texts of the various manuscripts. Here it is edited from Stockholm papp. 8vo nr 15 (A), which contains fewer errors than the other manuscripts, and variant readings are given from the best manuscript in the B group, B, and from C, D and E, that is Lbs 1562 4to, Stockholm papp. fol. nr 57, Thott 1491 4to and Lbs 1441 4to respectively.

PREVIOUS EDITIONS

Edda Sæmundar hinns fróda. Edda Rhytmica seu antiqvior, vulgo Sæmundina dicta I, København 1787, 199–232, is the first printed edition of *Hrafnagaldur*. There it is edited by Guðmundur Magnússon (1741–1798) from MS Icel. 47 (47), a manuscript edition made by Jón Eiríksson (1728–1787). 47 includes variant readings in the margin, and these were used in the printed edition's critical apparatus, which also made use of a manuscript that was in the possession of Geir Vídalín (1761–1823) and a commentary by Gunnar Pálsson (1714–1791) in AM 424 fol. It has not been possible to identify Geir Vídalín's manuscript among those that now survive. An account of the manuscript relationships is to be found in Guðmundur Magnússon's introduction (pp. xlii–xlvii).

In *Edda Sæmundar hinns fróda. Collectio carminum veterum scaldorum Sæmundiana dicta*, edited by Rasmus Kr. Rask and Arvid August Afzelius, Stockholm 1818, 88–92, Stockholm papp. 8vo nr 15 (A), Stockholm papp. fol. nr 34 (34) and Stockholm papp. fol. nr 46 (46) are used. Guðmundur Magnússon's edition of 1787 is used as well. There is an account of the manuscript relationships in Afzelius's introduction to the work (no page numbering).

In *Forspiallslióþ*, in the series *Bodsrit Bessastadaskóla*, Videyjar klaustri 1837, 24–29, edited by Hallgrímur Scheving, the text is based on Guðmundur Magnússon's edition of 1787 and Rask's of 1818.

In *Den ældre Edda. Samling af norrøne Oldkvad, indeholdende Nordens ældste Gude- og Helte-Sagn. Ved det akademiske Collegiums Foranstaltning udgivet efter de ældste og bedste Haandskrifter, og forsynet med fuldstændigt Variant-Apparat*, edited by P. A. Munch, Christiania 1847, 175–177, *Forspjallsljóþ* is put in an appendix without variants. Munch gives an account of the medieval manuscripts he has used in his work, but not of the later paper manuscripts, and so not of the manuscripts on which he based his edition of *Forspjallsljóþ*. His edition includes distinctive readings from both the A and B groups, and there are also emendations, so that it is difficult to see on which manuscript or manuscripts it is based.

In *Die Edda: Eine Sammlung altnordischer Götter- und Heldenlieder. Urschrift mit erklärenden Anmerkungen, Glossar und Einleitung, altnordischer Mythologie und Grammatik*, edited by Hermann Lüning, Zürich 1859, 516–524, the text is printed from P. A. Munch's edition of 1847, with occasional changes.

In *Edda Sæmundar hins fróða. Mit einem Anhang zum Theil bisher ungedruckter Gedichte*, edited by Theodor Möbius, Leipzig 1860, 216–

219, *Hrafnagaldur* is printed from P. A. Munch's edition of 1847, with a few changes.

In 1875 in Strassburg, Friedrich Wilh. Bergmann edited *Hrafnagaldur* with a German tanslation in *Weggewohnts Lied (Vegtams kvida), Der Odins Raben Orakelsang (Hrafna galdr Odins) und Der Seherin Voraussicht (Völu spâ). Drei Eschatologische Gedichte der Sæmunds-Edda*. There is no mention of which manuscript(s) or edition was used.

In *Norrœn fornkvæði. Islands samling af folkelige Oldtidsdigte om Nordens Guder og Heroer almindelig kaldet Sæmundar Edda hins fróða*, edited by Sophus Bugge, Christiania 1867, 371–376, no information is given about which manuscript formed the basis of his edition of *Hrafnagaldur*. It seems to be an improved version of Guðmundur Magnússon's and Rask's editions, collated with various additional manuscripts. An account is given of the manuscript relationships on pp. xlvi–xlix, liii and lvi–lvii. In connection with *Hrafnagaldur*, Bugge mentions readings from Jón Eiríksson's manuscript, 47, Geir Vídalín's manuscript and Gunnar Pálsson's commentary, which all seem to be derived from Guðmundur Magnússon's edition of 1787. In his text of *Hrafnagaldur* Bugge made use of A, C, NKS 1866 4to (1866), NKS 1108 fol. (1108), NKS 1109 fol. (1109) and NKS 1111 fol. (1111).

In Eysteinn Björnsson and William P. Reaves's edition of *Hrafnagaldur*, which was posted on the internet (http://notendur.hi.is/eybjorn/ugm/hrg/hrg.html) in 1998 and for the most part removed again in 2002, the text was to a large extent based on Bugge's edition of 1867, but 1109 was also used.[1]

In *Lesbók* in the Icelandic newspaper *Morgunblaðið*, 27/4 2002, *Hrafnagaldur* was edited by Jónas Kristjánsson from A.

DATE AND HISTORICAL CONTEXT

DATE

Already Guðmundur Magnússon regarded the poem as later than the other eddic poems. Since it is not transmitted in other than paper manuscripts, it could not, according to Guðmundur, have been composed by Sæmundr fróði or the author of the earliest collection of Eddic poems. Discussion

---

[1] Eysteinn Björnsson and Reaves's work on the poem led to the performance of the choral and orchestral work 'Hrafnagaldur Óðins' with music by Sigur Rós, Hilmar Örn Hilmarsson and Steindór Andersen at *Listahátíð í Reykjavík* 2002.

of the poem's age continued during the years after the first edition.[2] In his Danish translation of the eddic poems of 1821, the Icelandic professor in Copenhagen, Finnur Magnússon (1781–1847), argued in favour of *Hrafnagaldur*'s early date. Evidence for this is the poem's 'extremely ancient vocabulary, as well as its fragmentary nature, and in particular its genuine mythical spirit plus the fact that it only has very few allusions to stories known otherwise from eddas or sagas' (*Den ældre Edda* 1821–1823, II 210). Hallgrímur Scheving (1781–1861), on the other hand, considered the poem to be much later than the other eddic poems. He thought the poem had been written in Christian times by someone who knew Latin.[3] But since Munch's and Bugge's editions of the Edda of 1847 and 1867 respectively the general opinion has been that *Hrafnagaldur* must be regarded as postmedieval both on the grounds of its style and transmission. Nevertheless, Jónas Kristjánsson has recently put forward the thesis that the poem is from the Middle Ages and therefore should be reaccepted into the corpus of eddic poems, though it appears that he is not including it in his own forthcoming edition.

In his edition of the eddic poems of 1867, Bugge considered *Hrafnagaldur* to be a postmedieval antiquarian construction (*Norrœn fornkvæði* 1867, xlvi–xlvii):

> This poem ought in future to be excluded from collections of Old Norse mythical and heroic poems ... Forspjallsljóð ... is a learned poem, composed in later times by someone who was very familiar with, indeed well read in the ancient poems, and who had a bent for imitating the poetry of a long past age; it was probably from the very beginning recorded in writing.

Bugge states that while the eddic poems in general are difficult to understand because of their great age and the for us moderns alien material, *Hrafnagaldur* is hardly comprehensible because of its 'artificial'

---

[2] See Fidjestøl 1999, 58. Grundtvig was an advocate for the poem's great age in his *Nordens Mytologi* of 1808 (p. 8): '[The poem] is in general believed to be very late, both by reason of its style and because it is lacking in the earliest copies. This, however, proves nothing, since its style is even less like the modern than the ancient, and its close association with the Æsir points quite definitely to a genuine heathen as author.'

[3] Rask did not express an opinion about the age of the poem, but in his edition placed it in front of *Baldrs draumar*, whereby he seems to support Gunnar Pálsson's hypothesis that *Hrafnagaldur* formed an introduction to that poem. Afzelius discusses *Hrafnagaldur* together with, among others, *Vǫluspá*, *Grímnismál*, *Vafþrúðnismál* and *Baldrs draumar*, which suggests that he took the poem to be of a similar age.

expressions and 'far-fetched' images (xlvii).[4] After this, Bugge on linguistic grounds concludes about the poem's lateness (xlvi–xlvii):[5]

> A poem, whose author's relationship to the ancient language is such, cannot in my view be from the Middle Ages at all, but must be from a later time. I believe that it is no older than the seventeenth century.

Bugge's rejection of *Hrafnagaldur*'s authenticity as a medieval poem is consistent with and an emphatic endorsement of an attitude that P. A. Munch expressed in his edition of the eddic poems, where he wrote (*Den ældre Edda* 1847, x–xi):

> It cannot, however, be denied that the major part of the rest, and other things, too, that are found in paper manuscripts of the Edda, have a rather suspicious look. This applies especially to Grógaldr and Hrafnagaldr Óðins . . . These . . . are therefore omitted from the series of eddic poems proper, and only added in an appendix.

What could count against Munch's and Bugge's interpretation of the poem's date is Árni Magnússon's mention of the poem in a letter to Jón Halldórsson (1665–1736), rural dean in Hítardalur, dated 18/6 1729, in which he asks to be sent copies that had been made earlier of documents that he had lost in the fire of 1728. Árni says that he had owned copies of eddic poems ('Sæm(undar) Eddur') that had been destroyed in the fire. He lacks *Hrafnagaldur*, *Grougaldur* and *Heiðreks gátur*, which were supposed to have been included in manuscripts of eddic poems that Brynjólfur Sveinsson (1605–1675) had been responsible for. According to Árni, these poems had existed in copies of a copy made by Þorsteinn Eyjólfsson at Háeyri (c. 1645–1714), of which Árni himself had owned two that were burnt in 1728. Þorsteinn studied at the school of Skálholt where he finished his education no later than 1668. In the years 1682–1684, he was baliff there. In his letter, Árni further writes (*Bréf Árna Magnússonar* 1975, 147):

---

[4] Already in the seventeenth century the poem was renowned for being largely impenetrable. See Guðmundur Magnússon in *Edda* 1787–1828, I 204.

[5] Bugge mentions as an example that *hveim* is used as a relative pronoun in st. 13. But *hveim* is also found in *Baldrs draumar* 6/5, which is preserved in a manuscript from about 1300. Bugge thinks there is a string of words that were inspired by Snorri's *Edda* and *Vǫluspá*, among others *hǫrgr* (st. 20) and *hárbaðmr* (st. 7). *Hárbaðmr*, according to Bugge, seems to be used because the author of *Hrafnagaldur* read *hárbaðmr* in *Vǫluspá* in the Codex Regius as one word and misunderstood it to mean 'hair tree'. The best manuscripts of *Hrafnagaldur*, however, have *harðbaðmr*, not *hárbaðmr*. Bugge points out that *máttkat* (st. 2) is a grammatical error on the part of the author, who had misunderstood ancient word forms. In addition, he claims that the genitive *-þollar* (st. 25) must be a case of misunderstanding of an earlier form, since 'the genitive of *þollr* is *þolls*' (xlvii).

Eg hafde (sem brann) bref Sal. Sra Olafs (Skolameistara ockar) ahrærande eina af þessum odis (mig minnir Hrafnag. Odins) ad Mag. Brÿniolfur hafe þá qvidu uppskrifa láted epter gömlu saurugu einstaka blade, og minnir mig þar stæde, ad þar aptan vid hefde vantad, og eins kynne um fleira geingid vera. Þetta verdur so sem allt i þoku, þvi documentenn eru burtu.

Gísli Brynjúlfsson had drawn Bugge's attention to this letter, which had been printed in *Kjöbenhavns Universitets-Journal* 4, 1796, 8 in a Danish translation by Skúli Thorlacius, but Bugge did not think that one could trust it (see *Norrœn fornkvæði* 1867, xlviii). In his letter, Árni mentions the reference by Síra Ólafur Jónsson (1637–1688) to Brynjólfur Sveinsson's having had *Hrafnagaldur* copied from a single old and dirty leaf, and this presents the possibility that the poem could date from the Middle Ages,[6] and that the leaf could have held the author's autograph.[7] Árni Magnússon was, however, not certain that the poem referred to was *Hrafnagaldur*, and he had not himself seen the supposedly old and dirty leaf. After the fire of 1728 'all this has become as it were in a fog, for the documents have gone', he writes. Even if Árni remembered the contents of the letter correctly, this does not necessarily carry much weight as evidence, because as Árni himself demonstrates clearly in his study of Sæmundr fróði from 1690 (*Vita Sæmundi multiscii*), Brynjólfur and his contemporaries were poor judges of the origins and antiquity of eddic poetry, mainly because of their groundless assumptions that the poems of the Codex Regius were only a small part of a vast collection originally compiled by Sæmundr Sigfússon (died 1133). This may also have made Brynjólfur and those working for him more prone to accept 'new discoveries' of ancient poetry uncritically, since they were expecting further poems to turn up from

[6] This is also, moreover, Bugge's attitude to the poem elsewhere in his edition of the *Edda*, where he writes that *Hrafnagaldur* may be a late medieval poem (*Norrœn fornkvæði* 1867, 140). Cf. Jónas Kristjánsson in *Hrafnagaldur Óðins* 2002, 6.

[7] Árni presumably wrote the letter to Jón Halldórsson because Ólafur Jónsson was Jón's paternal uncle, hoping that Jón possessed a copy of the old and dirty leaf. Ólafur, moreover, was principal at the school at Skálholt when Guðmundur Ólafsson, who brought A to Stockholm, and Ásgeir Jónsson, who wrote B, were studying there. They would probably have heard Ólafur tell the story of the leaf on which *Hrafnagaldur* was written that Brynjólfur had had copied, and it was probably the main reason for their making or acquiring copies of the poem. Ólafur first started teaching in Skálholt in 1659 and was principal from 1667 to 1683. He was still principal when Árni himself studied there (from 1680 to 1683), but one may surmise, given the content of the letter, that Árni only received information about *Hrafnagaldur* from Ólafur via his letter to him. This letter must have been written before Ólafur's death on the 24th of September 1688, and probably after Árni started working as Bartholin's assistant in 1684.

this vast hypothetical collection. We cannot therefore know whether this information can be trusted or not. Árni seemed to remember that it said in the letter that the end of the poem was missing.[8] The poem, however, as we have it, begins and ends with complete stanzas, which speaks against its having been fragmentarily preserved. There are also good arguments based on the content that both the beginning and end of the poem are preserved. This question is discussed below (p. 23).

The poem consists of 26 eight-line stanzas. For comparison there are 16·5 stanzas of *Vǫluspá* on the recto of the first leaf of the Codex Regius of the eddic poems (GKS 2365 4to). It is thus not impossible for the 26 stanzas of *Hrafnagaldur* to have been written on one leaf of a manuscript or on one sheet of about the same size as the leaves in GKS 2365 4to. The poems in the Codex Regius are not divided into stanzas, whereas most manuscripts containing *Hrafnagaldur* are. But in a note in D it is mentioned that the text it was copied from was written out continuously (as prose). In two of the earliest manuscripts, A and B, each stanza is written as a single paragraph of prose, but both scribes make the same mistake in the stanza division in stt. 20–21, attaching the first half of st. 21 to st. 20, leaving the second half of st. 22 as a short stanza. This mistake is likely to have been in a manuscript from which both A and B were derived, which could have been the one used by Brynjólfur Sveinsson for his copy. Even if the supposedly old and dirty leaf with *Hrafnagaldur* on it really existed, there is no knowing how old it actually was. Árni Magnússon's description of the leaf as old stems via Síra Ólafur Jónsson from a phrase apparently used by Brynjólfur, so his statement cannot be used to support a medieval dating of the poem. It is my conclusion that the letter cannot be used as evidence for the poem's early origin or date in the face of weighty arguments for its lateness. But the letter gives valuable information in that it connects the poem with the scholarly activity in Skálholt in the days of Brynjólfur.

If the copies of *Hrafnagaldur* stem from a single leaf not containing any other poems, one might suppose that in copies of this leaf the poem would end up in various textual contexts. In some manuscripts we find the poem placed after *Sólarljóð* and before *Vǫluspá*, after which there follow

---

[8] The first editor of the poem, Guðmundur Magnússon, thought in fact that the poem lacked both beginning and end, while Finnur Magnússon in his translation of the eddic poems (*Den ældre Edda*, 1821–1823, II 209 and 213) thought that a part of the poem had been lost. In the missing stanzas it was imagined that an explanation of the poem's otherwise hardly intelligible main title might be found. Apparently neither Guðmundur Magnússon nor Finnur Magnússon knew of Árni Magnússon's letter.

the rest of the eddic poems in the Codex Regius.⁹ This is the case in A and (probably originally) in B, which are two of the earliest manuscripts. The archetype of these manuscripts would presumably have had the poems in this order. C has the poem between *Hallmundar ljóð* and *Hákonar saga Hákonarsonar*. In D, *Hrafnagaldur* comes after the Codex Regius poems and *Grottasǫngr, Gróugaldur, Fjölsvinnsmál, Hyndluljóð* (see Bugge's discussion of the placing of *Hrafnagaldur, Norrœn fornkvœði* 1867, xlix). In E *Hrafnagaldur* comes between *Fjölsvinnsmál* and *Grottasǫngr*. Both D and E are copies made in the eighteenth century, and they seem clearly more remote from the original than the other three manuscripts that have text-critical value.

Common readings in A, B, C, D and E (among others 'Frygg' 23/7 — though here E has 'Frigg' — and 'dys' 6/2) show that they, and presumably their archetype, must stem from the seventeenth century,[10] and as regards the various placings of the poem, it could be a case of different antiquarians' choices of a poetical context.

It may be added that manuscripts deriving from Brynjólfur Sveinsson's principal copyist Jón Erlendsson of Villingaholt (died 1672) are not exact copies, as can be seen from his copies of *Íslendingabók* and *Arons saga* (see Jón Jóhannesson 1956, viii). In his edition of *Guðmundar sögur biskups* I (1983), Stefán Karlsson compared the end of *Arons saga* in AM 551 d β 4to with Jón Erlendsson's copy of this manuscript (AM 212 fol.). Stefán concluded that 'Jón's manuscript . . . shows signs that the original had already been damaged and was in some passages difficult to read, and Jón's text is often corrupt and in some places incomprehensible' (Stefán Karlsson 1983, clx). It is impossible to know whether it was Jón Erlendsson that made the copy of *Hrafnagaldur* for Brynjólfur Sveinsson that Árni Magnússon referred to in his letter. It is known that Jón Ólafsson of Grunnavík (1705–1779) had possessed two manuscripts of eddic poems, of which one, which he had got from Páll Sveinsson, had been

---

⁹ When *Sólarljóð* stands at the head of many of the earliest collections of eddic poems, it is probably because it was believed that Sæmundr fróði had composed it. In Jón Árnason's *Íslenzkar þjóðsögur* (1954–1961, I 475) we find an abbreviated statement from a manuscript, AM 254 8vo (p. 346), that is dated to the end of the seventeenth century: 'Sæmundur andaðist 1133, en með hverjum atburðum höfum vær eigi heyrt, þó segja menn, að hann þridagaður hafi úr líkrekkjunni risið og þá kveðið þá drápu, er hans ljóða-Eddu er vön að fylgja og kallast Sólarljóð.' See also Bjarni Einarsson 1955, cv–cvi.

[10] The earliest examples of *i, í* and *ei* being written for *y, ý* and *ey* or vice versa are from the end of the period 1400–1550 (Stefán Karlsson 2000, 55; 2004, 50), but it becomes common only in the seventeenth century.

written by Jón Erlendsson. Jón Ólafsson had this manuscript sent to him in Copenhagen in 1727, but the ship sank (see Jón Helgason 1926, 287). In his article in *Lesbók Morgunblaðsins* 27/4 2002, Jónas Kristjánsson dates *Hrafnagaldur* to the fourteenth century. He uses Árni Magnússon's letter as support for his assumption that the poem is ancient. According to Jónas, a lot of words and sentences in *Hrafnagaldur* derive from *Vǫluspá* in the Codex Regius.[11] The many errors in copies of the poem are supposed to have arisen at two stages, 1) in the course of the poem's oral transmission, and 2) in the copying of 'an old, dirty leaf'.

On the grounds of the influence of *Vǫluspá*, the origin of which he dates to around AD 1000, Jónas Kristjánsson sets a terminus post quem for *Hrafnagaldur* of that year. But it may be pointed out that the influence of *Vǫluspá* does not of course preclude a late date. If the author of *Hrafnagaldur* found himself in the milieu of Brynjólfur Sveinsson in Skálholt, it is by no means improbable that he knew the Codex Regius of the eddic poems, which came into Brynjólfur's possession in 1643. Already in 1665 the first eddic poems appeared in print in Resen's editions, namely *Vǫluspá* and *Hávamál*. The author need not have used these editions, but they were both an example of and a contribution to the sudden celebrity and dissemination of the eddic poems in learned circles in the seventeenth century.

Hrafnagaldur cannot, according to Jónas Kristjánsson, have been composed before about 1300. He puts forward as evidence that the metre of the poem would be destroyed if the svarabhakti vowel in nominative singular masculine endings were left out. The svarabhakti vowel is not found in manuscripts from before the thirteenth century.

Kristján Árnason contradicted Jónas Kristjánsson's dating of *Hrafnagaldur* in an article in *Lesbók Morgunblaðsins* 25/5 2002, on the basis of an examination of syllable length in *Hrafnagaldur*. Kristján found seven lines in the poem that break the metrical rules in relation to the old vowel

---

[11] Jónas considers the following to have been taken from *Vǫluspá* in the Codex Regius: st. 1: elur íviðjur < *Vsp.* 2: níu íviðjur; st. 5: Vitið enn, eða hvat? < *Vsp.*'s repeated: Vituð ér enn, eða hvat?; st. 7: hárðbaðms (or hárbaðms) < *Vsp.* 19: hár baðmr (but cf. footnote 5 above); st. 12: Né mun mælti, né mál knátti < *Vsp.* 5: Sól þat né vissi . . . stjǫrnur þat né vissi . . . máni þat né vissi; st. 13: Einn kemur austan < *Vsp.* 50: Hrymr ekr austan; st. 13: mæran of Miðgarð < *Vsp.* 4: þeir er Miðgarð mæran skópu; st. 19: sjót Sæhrímni saddist rakna < *Vsp.* 41: rýðr ragna sjǫt rauðum dreyra; st. 23: gengu frá gildi, | goðin kvǫddu < *Vsp.* 23: Þá gengu regin ǫll | á rǫkstóla . . . eða skyldu goðin ǫll | gildi eiga; st. 25: Jǫrmungrundar | í jódýr nyrðra < *Vsp.* 5: Sól varp sunnan | sinni Mána | hendi inni hœgri | of himin jódýr. To which I would add st. 5: Lopti með lævi < *Vsp.* 25: lopt allt lævi blandit.

quantity system, and his conclusion runs that it is improbable, if not downright impossible, for the poem in its transmitted form to be from the fourteenth century, before the changes in Icelandic syllable quantity which did not begin until the sixteenth century (Kristján Árnason 2002, 11). There are, however, many stanzas that do not offend the metrical rules, so Kristján suggests that the stanzas of the poem might be from different periods, and that they could have been put together in the seventeenth century at the earliest.[12] The poem, however, seems to have a coherent content, so that it seems improbable that its stanzas could be from different periods.

An examination of the surviving manuscripts of *Hrafnagaldur* shows that there are only minor disagreements between the word forms and spellings in them. The poem includes archaising spellings, among other things often, but not consistently, omitting the svarabhakti vowel. That people were capable of archaising the language in the eighteenth century is apparent from the late poem *Gunnarsslagur*. It is transmitted in among other places NKS 1877 4to, where it is introduced with the words: 'Ein af þeim töpuðu kviðum | Sæmundar-Eddu'. Guðmundur Magnússon discovered the poem while on a journey in Iceland in 1780 and published it in the Arnamagnæan edition of the eddic poems (*Edda* 1787–1828, II xxiv and 1001–1010). In the introduction to the second volume of *Edda* 1787–1828, Børge Thorlacius mentions a rumour that Gunnar Pálsson was the author of *Gunnarsslagur*. But according to a letter from Árni Þorsteinsson in Norðurmúlasýsla to Guttormur Pálsson, Guðmundur Magnússon had found the poem in a manuscript which was a copy of an old manuscript. Árni owned this manuscript and had received it from Skafti Skaftason, who had said that the thirteen eddic poems in it were copied from an old original previously in the possession of Sigurður Eiríksson, priest at Skeggjastaðir on Langanesströnd (died 1768). If, Thorlacius writes, *Gunnarsslagur* was in this manuscript, Gunnar could not be its author. Árni, however, also states that his son had seen the poem in a collection of Gunnar Pálsson's poetry (*Edda* 1787–1828 II, xxv–xxvi). Thorlacius notes that late paper manuscripts, badly treated, can absorb smoke and humidity and thus delude inexperienced eyes about their antiquity (xxvii). The language

---

[12] This hypothesis agrees on some points with the Danish writer and translator Bertel Christian Sandvig's supposition that the poem 'consists of nothing but incoherent passages that a lover of the art of poetry has excerpted from a larger poem' (1783–1785, I 4r–4v). Aðalheiður Guðmundsdóttir (2001, cxxiv, cciv) has looked at the werewulf motif in st. 8. She has not proposed a date for *Hrafnagaldur*, but has pointed out that this motif in the poem is reminiscent of passages in other Old Norse texts.

and vocabulary of *Gunnarsslagur* are archaised (which is also the case in Gunnar Pálsson's autograph in JS 273 4to), and it is presented as a medieval poem,[13] but it was nevertheless composed by Gunnar Pálsson in 1745.[14] Another example is *Hafgeirs saga Flateyings* from the eighteenth century.[15] Confirmation that this saga is a product of the eighteenth century, according to Peter Jorgensen, is the use of the adjective *þankafullur* (probably from Danish *tankefuld* or German *gedankenvoll*), which is not common in Icelandic. The word appears in the dictionary compiled by Jón Ólafsson of Grunnavík during the years 1734 to 1779 that is preserved in AM 433 fol.[16] Even though an old historiographer could be deceived by this saga, it is obviously an example of a late imitation of the ancient sagas.

[13] Examples of archaisation are the omission of the svarabhakti vowel, 'vá' instead of 'vo' and 'e' instead of 'i' in inflexions.

[14] See *Edda* 1787–1828, II xxiv–xxvii and Bugge's remarks in *Norrœn fornkvæði* 1867, xlix: 'Any doubts [about the authorship] are dispelled by the information imparted to me by Guðbrandr Vigfússon: Gunnarsslagr is found in Kvæðasafn síra Gunnars Pálssonar in British Museum 11,192 (not an autograph), and there the author himself (after 1777) has written about this poem: "Eg sendi þetta nýsmíðað þeim nafnkenda manni séra Eyjólfi á Völlum, er lét vel yfir og lagði þetta til síðast: jubeo te macte esse tanto in antiquitatibus nostris profectu; og ætla eg þetta hafi verið 1745–1746. Sveini lögmanni sendi eg og exemplar . . . er mitt litla verk vel approberaði. Framar man eg eigi af að segja, enda máské tortýndr sé sá verki, þar mag. Hálfdan Einarsson hans eigi getr í sinni sciagraphia hist. lit., en nefner þó aðra mína smákveðlinga. G.P.S."' Gunnar Pálsson's autograph is probably to be found in JS 273 4to a II 7. In connection with his BA assignment at Háskóli Íslands 2008, Haukur Þorgeirsson discovered Eyjólfur Jónsson's letter in reply to Gunnar Pálsson about *Gunnarsslagur*, dated 23. September 1745 (ÍBR 120 8vo, pp. 204–205; see Haukur Þorgeirsson 2008, 24; on the autograph, p. 29). Even though the poet did not pretend that the poem was ancient, it was still soon apprehended as such. In the same letter Eyjólfur Jónsson actually wrote that if he had not known better, he would have believed that the poem was one of the medieval eddic poems.

[15] Peter Jorgensen (1977) says that an Icelandic student in Copenhagen, Þorlákur Magnússon Ísfiord (c. 1748–1781), wrote this saga during the years 1774 to 1776, claimed it was copied fom a thirteenth-century manuscript and probably sold it to the elderly and by that time half blind Bernhard Møllmann (1702–1778), professor at Copenhagen University, royal historiographer and librarian at the Royal Library in Copenhagen, who was also, incidentally, in 1755 trying to obtain a good copy of the eddic poems in connection with the Arnamagnæan Commission's plans to publish Snorri's *Edda* (see Jón Helgason 1926, 286).

[16] See the list of words in his dictionary on the website of *Orðabók Háskólans*: http://www.lexis.hi.is/JOL_skra.htm. *Þankafullur* is found later on in *rímur* too (see *Orðabók Háskólans*: http://lexis.hi.is/cgi-bin/ritmal/leitord.cgi).

Hrafnagaldur also contains a loanword which can give a clue to the poem's age, or at least to a terminus post quem. In st. 20 the Middle Low German loanword *máltíð* is found, which according to Veturliði Óskarsson is not used regularly in Icelandic before 1500 (see Lassen 2006, 557). It appears in an Icelandic document from 1380 and occasionally in manuscripts between c. 1350 and c. 1530, among other places in a manuscript containing *Bárðar saga Snæfellsáss* and in Flateyjarbók (Veturliði Óskarsson 2003, 281). The use of the word in *Hrafnagaldur* suggests that the poem was not written before the middle of the fourteenth century. But it can hardly be as old as that. This is indicated by, among other things, the use of the words 'virt', which is not recorded in *Orðabók Háskólans* from before the sixteenth century, and 'larður' or 'laraður', which are not found earlier than the seventeenth century (see the commentary to stt. 18 and 23).

Nótt skal nema nýræða til

In st. 22 of *Hrafnagaldur* what looks like a proverb, 'Nótt skal nema nýræða til', appears. The proverb sheds light on the date of the poem, so we shall now discuss where it comes from.

In 1843 Hallgrímur Scheving, one of the early editors of *Hrafnagaldur*, published a collection of Icelandic proverbs in *Bodsrit Bessastadaskóla* ('Islendskir málshættir safnadir, útvaldir og í stafrófsrød færdir af Skólakennara Dr. H. Scheving'), in which he includes (p. 38) 'Nótt skal nema nýræða til', but the only occurrence he quotes is that in *Hrafnagaldur*. Bjarni Vilhjálmsson and Óskar Halldórsson's *Íslenskir málshættir* (1979) include 'Nótt skal nema til nýræða', but their only reference is to Scheving.

The earliest medieval example of a proverb that means that night should be used for taking counsel is in Michaelis Apostolius (c. 1422–1480), who in his Greek proverb collection Παροιμίαι (Paroemiæ) mentions ἐν νυκτὶ βουλή. Michaelis Apostolius was a collector of manuscripts and was located in Italy. This work of his was translated into Latin by Petrus Pantinus and published in Leiden in 1619 in an edition by the famous Dutch humanist Daniel Heinsius (1580–1655), and here the proverb is rendered 'in nocte consilium'. The most influential collection of proverbs in Europe in the Renaissance period was, however, Erasmus of Rotterdam's *Adagia*. Guðmundur Magnússon, in his commentary on *Hrafnagaldur* (*Edda* 1787–1828, I 227, note) identified 'Nótt skal nema nýræða til' with the Greco-Roman proverb 'in nocte consilium', referring to the relevant place in Erasmus's work, and concluded that the proverb was also known in the North.

Erasmus's work is a key to the understanding of European culture in the sixteenth century. It was based on among other things Michaelis

Apostolius's collection of proverbs, the primary dissemination of which was via Erasmus. The latter's collection first appeared in Paris in 1500 under the title *Veterum maximeque insignium paroemiarum id est adagiorum collectanea*, and was reissued in revised forms in 1508 (Venice), 1515 (Basel) and thereafter several more times. It also soon came out in translations into among other languages German (Georgius Spalatinus: *Man muß entweder ein konig oder aber ein narr geborn werden*, 1520) and English (Richard Taverner: *Proverbes or adagies*, 1539). The earliest editions were just a small selection of proverbs compared with the later ones, which were expanded, corrected and revised.

The proverb in *Hrafnagaldur* is found already in some of the earliest editions of Erasmus's *Adagia*, which was disseminated enormously widely in its various editions, and after Erasmus's death the work continued to be expanded. There was a copy of the 1599 edition in the library of Brynjólfur Sveinsson, and this is now in Landsbókasafn Íslands (see Jón Helgason 1948, 140; *Ritaukaskrá Landsbókasafnsins* 1926, 60). This printed edition is considerably earlier than the earliest manuscripts that contain *Hrafnagaldur*. In Brynjólfur's copy, 'Noctu urgenda consilia' and 'Nox dabit consilium' are given on pp. 328–329, and 'In nocte consilium' on p. 508. The *Adagia* was also known in Iceland earlier in the sixteenth century. Magnús prúði Jónsson (1525–1591) compiled a rhymed collection of proverbs that was partly based on the *Adagia*, though the collection as a whole is not a translation from Latin (see Grímur M. Helgason 1961). It is preserved in JS 391 8vo, which has a reference to Erasmus on p. 107, and Lbs 1199 4to, though the proverb in *Hrafnagaldur* is not found here.

According to the *Adagia*, the proverb 'noctu urgenda consilium' is of Greek origin, and no earlier Latin example is quoted. Erasmus (1599, 328) says his principal source was a school book from the second century AD, Theon's Progymnasmata (εν νυκτι βουλεσ εχεσθαι). He also mentions examples from Sophocles, Plutarch and an anonymous Greek writer. Finally, he gives a French example ('Gallicum proverbium'), 'la nuict a conseil'. Under 'In nocte consilium' he mentions a commonplace among the uneducated ('ab idiotis nostratibus') 'super hac re indormiam ('I shall sleep on it'), and here he refers to Plutarch.

In *Proverbes Français antérieurs au XVe siècle* (Morawski 1925, ix) we find 'la nuit a conseil', for which a fifteenth-century manuscript in the Vatican (Reg. 1429) is given as a source. This manuscript contains proverbs and legal commentaries, and the collection may have been compiled before 1444. In the fifteenth century, Greek antiquity was rediscovered, and learned Greeks came to Italy, France and Spain (Michaelis Apostolius was one of these learned Greeks in Italy). The proverb does not seem to belong to any earlier French tradition, and moreover there does not seem to have been any connection between France and Iceland in the fifteenth century either.

In *Lateinische Sprichwörter und Sentenzen des Mittelalters* (Walther 1963–1969) we find: 'Visum campus habet, nemus aurem, consilium nox' (33811a).[17] This is taken from the fifteenth-century British Museum manuscript Harl. 3362.

It is unlikely that the proverb was known in Iceland direct from Michaelis Apostolius's collection or from the Greek examples that are mentioned in the *Adagia*, or that it reached Iceland via France or England in the fifteenth century. I have found references to the proverb in only one manuscript in each of these two countries, so it cannot have been widespread there. It is reasonable to assume that both these examples go back to Michaelis Apostolius.[18]

The proverb must, however, have reached Iceland via Erasmus's *Adagia*. It is after all not recorded in medieval Icelandic texts; the earliest example is in *Hrafnagaldur*. It is also found in Latin in the seventeenth century in Brynjólfur Sveinsson's library, which was unique in Iceland. Brynjólfur had probably brought the book with him from Copenhagen when he returned to Iceland in 1638. The proverb became so widespread in the Renaissance that scholars talk of the 'in nocte consilium topos' (Parkin 2006). Erasmus's proverb collection can thus provide a terminus post quem for *Hrafnagaldur*. The proverb 'nótt skal nema nýræða til' constitutes a high point in the poem towards its conclusion, and it is hard to imagine its having been added by a scribe who could not read what stood in an obscure and difficult original.

Hrafnagaldur apparently existed some time before the earliest preserved manuscripts that contain it. Guðmundur Magnússon tells us (*Edda* 1787–1828, I 204) that the Icelandic poet Eiríkur Hallsson at Höfði (1614–1698) spent ten years trying to understand the poem, after which he moreover threw it from him saying that he still only understood a little of it.

---

[17] In spite of the title, examples in this work are taken from both medieval and postmedieval texts. It also includes 'Semper consilium portat nox humida secum' (27920a) and 'In nocte consilium atra invenies candidum' (11898a). The sources of these are *Philosophia Patrum* 2887, 2888.

[18] The Danish proverbs that have a similar meaning are all later than Erasmus's *Adagia*. Compare 'Herr Iver i Boeslundes ordsprog (Sørensen 1980, 105), written between 1652 and 1684 (Sørensen 1980, 58). Erasmus's and Michaelis's proverb collections are mentioned in Peder Syv's proverb bibliography in Rostgaard 48 8vo (Sørensen 1988, 431–433).

This means that Eiríkur started studying the poem in 1688 at the latest, and probably earlier, since Guðmundur does not say that Eiríkur died immediately after abandoning it, and he can hardly have begun work on it as soon as it was written. So *Hrafnagaldur* may have been composed around the middle of the seventeenth century, and would then have been connected with the Renaissance in Iceland, the rediscovery of the Codex Regius in 1643 and the learned circle around Brynjólfur Sveinsson, who was bishop at Skálholt. Some of the earliest known people to have made or acquired copies of the poem are, as mentioned above, Guðmundur Ólafsson and Ásgeir Jónsson, who studied in Skálholt from 1673 to 1677 and from 1674 to 1678 respectively. It may be considered likely that the poem was actually composed at Skálholt. It may therefore appear surprising that it so quickly gained the reputation of being ancient, but that such a thing is possible is shown by the case of *Gunnarsslagur* (see p. 16 above); and this reputation may have given rise to the earliest copying activity involving *Hrafnagaldur*, which was perhaps initiated by Brynjólfur.

To explain why reports of *Hrafnagaldur* first surface in the northern diocese of Hólar (Eiríkur Hallsson at Höfði) and from students in the southern diocese of Skálholt (Guðmundur Ólafsson and Ásgeir Jónsson) one might suspect the involvement of Þórður Þorláksson, who was the son of Þorlákur Skúlason, bishop of Hólar (died 1656) and brother of Gísli Þorláksson, Þorlákur's successor as bishop of Hólar (1656–1684). Þórður studied in Denmark and Germany, and travelled to France, Belgium and the Netherlands. After he succeeded Brynjólfur Sveinsson as bishop of Skálholt in 1674, he brought the Hólar press to Skálholt where he initiated the printing of medieval sagas. Þórður Þorláksson was very active in collecting manuscripts and renewed the antiquarian activities in Skálholt (cf. Már Jónsson 1998, 189–190). Ólafur Jónsson was principal at the school at Skálholt during the last years of Brynjólfur Sveinsson's and the first years of Þórður Þorláksson's bishopric. Þórður may have heard about the single leaf containing *Hrafnagaldur* and the rumour of it may have reached the north of Iceland via him.

THE TITLE HRAFNAGALDUR ÓÐINS/FORSPJALLSLJÓÐ

The main title, *Hrafnagaldur Óðins*, seems to be a misunderstanding, for Óðinn's ravens play no part in the poem.[19] It is possible that the poem was originally nameless, and at a very early stage was given the title 'Hrafnagaldur Óðins' due to a misunderstanding of 'hugur' in the third

[19] In his commentary in AM 424 fol., Gunnar Pálsson argued that *Hrafnagaldur* could be a misunderstanding of *hræfvagaldur*, which he then links to *valgaldr* in *Baldrs draumar* (*Edda* 1787–1828, I, 199).

stanza as an alternative form of the name 'Huginn' for one of Óðinn's ravens, parallel to the alternative forms Ullr/Ullinn and perhaps Óðr/Óðinn. The title should probably be interpreted to mean 'Song of Óðinn's ravens' and understood in connection with *Gylfaginning* ch. 38, *SnE* I 32/32–36. Cf. also the poems entitled 'Hrafnsmál' attributed to Þorbjǫrn hornklofi, Þormóðr Trefilsson and Sturla Þórðarson.

All manuscripts that contain *Hrafnagaldur* include the subtitle 'Forspjallsljóð', sometimes preceded by 'al.' or 'eþur'. The use of the noun 'forspjall' shows that the subtitle cannot stem from the Middle Ages. Fritzner's *Ordbog* does not include the word *forspjall*, but gives the meaning 'Tale, Fortælling' for the noun *spjall*. *Forspjall* is not included in *ONP*'s word list either (http://dataonp.hum.ku.dk/index.html). The earliest example that is given in *Orðabók Háskólans* is from 1649, in a verse in the *Ævidrápa* of Jón lærði Guðmundsson (1574–1658): 'Forspjall lítið | framan til ljóða | fyrir lesandann | eg læt hér vera'. The first twenty stanzas in his *Ævidrápa* comprise an introductory poem of a more general character than the decidedly autobiographical stanzas that follow. 'Forspjall' ('preface') is used by Jón lærði in a sense that seems identical to that of the Latin 'prologus', of which it is probably a translation. Jón belonged to the learned circle around Brynjólfur Sveinsson and was one of the Icelanders who copied medieval manuscripts and compiled commentaries on the ancient literature of Iceland, among other things making a copy of the Codex Upsaliensis of Snorri's *Edda* and writing notes on *Vǫluspá* and *Hávamál* (see Faulkes 1977, 77, 89; Einar G. Pétursson 1998, 133–134). The context in which Jón Guðmundsson used the word *forspjall* is similar to that in *Hrafnagaldur*, but perhaps in the latter it applies particularly to the first stanza, in which the poet gives an overview of the status of various beings. Thus Hallgrímur Scheving (1837, 7) in fact suggested that the title 'Forspjallsljóð', which can mean a preface in verse, applied exclusively to st. 1 of *Hrafnagaldur*.

The subtitle 'Forspjallsljóð' could have been inspired by Jón Guðmundsson's *Ævidrápa* (even if we cannot exclude the possibility of the relationship having been the reverse), but there is no reason why an existing, possibly untitled poem at some stage in its transmission should not have been given a later title, or possibly had the subtitle 'Forspjallsljóð' added. In an Edda manuscript that Gunnar Pálsson possessed, Páll Vídalín (1667–1727) is said to have written by *Hrafnagaldur*: 'það er Forspjallsljód' (Scheving 1837, 5; cf. also *Edda* 1787–1828, I 200). Scheving wrote in the commentary to his edition that Gunnar Pálsson did not know whether Vídalín was the first to call *Hrafnagaldur* by this name. Gunnar wrote a commentary to *Hrafnagaldur* which is preserved in AM 424 fol., and sent it to the poem's first editor Guðmundur Magnússon in Copenhagen. Even though Vídalín could not (on account of his age) have been the originator of the subtitle, it could be that it was not originally thought of as a title, but as a description, 'this is an introductory poem'. This description could afterwards have become attached to the title.

It is tempting to wonder whether the poem could have been written as a preface to one of the many collections of eddic poems that were made after 1643. In A and B the poem stands after *Sólarljóð* and before *Vǫluspá*. *Sólarljóð* could have gained its prominent position first in the collection because it was thought in the seventeenth century to have been composed by Sæmundr fróði (see note 9 above). *Hrafnagaldur* could have been placed next because it was thought of as a preface in verse to Sæmundr's *Edda*.

CONTENT AND STYLE

The *Hrafnagaldur* poet seems to have had a penchant for repetition of words within the same half-stanza, a kind of symmetrical ornamentation that gives his poem a baroque flavour (see for example stt. 3.5–8 and 4. 5–8). The content of the poem points to a date of composition later than that of genuinely medieval eddic poems. The action takes place among the gods just before Ragnarǫk, and describes Óðinn's vain attempt to gain knowledge of the future or to find a way out for the gods. The introductory stanza gives an overview of various beings in the world of the gods (Alfǫðr, Vanir, nornir, Æsir, etc) and shows the attitudes of various groups in the Norse mythological world towards the larger scheme of the gods' future. It serves to introduce the atmosphere for the poem's narrative, like the first stanza of *Hamðismál*, which indicates that the opening is preserved. It would appear that the conclusion of the narrative is also preserved,[20] for it ends with the day breaking and Heimdallur beginning to blow his horn, which according to Snorri's *Edda* sounds precisely when Ragnarǫk is imminent. The poem thus ends on a tragic climax. Even though it is not stated, it is clear that the gods are now going to meet their fate.

In this poem the future is not introduced, as is the case in *Vǫluspá* and *Baldrs draumar*. The journey to seek a prophecy or wise saying and the ominous dream have similarities to those in other eddic poems, but in contrast

[20] Guðmundur Magnússon thought (*Edda* 1787–1828, I 203), as mentioned above (note 8), that both beginning and end were lacking. His arguments for the end being missing were 1) that nothing is said about Bragi's departure from the prophetess, 2) that there is no information about the Æsir's further attempts to get something out of the prophetess, and 3) that it would have been natural, if Bragi had had no luck in getting the prophetess to speak, for Óðinn to have taken matters into his own hands.

to those poems the gods gain no information here from their journey. In the prophetic eddic poems there is a tragic element to the knowledge that Óðinn gains. In *Vǫluspá* Ragnarǫk is conjured up, in *Baldrs draumar* Baldr's death. But we do not see how the gods react to these events in those poems. We do see that, however, in *Hrafnagaldur*: Iðunn begins to weep, and the impotent gods know no way out of the problems that have apparently caused the weeping and which they themselves do not know about. In spite of the terrible portents of the future, they still sit in merry carousal towards the close of the poem. The parallels with *Vǫluspá* indicate that *Hrafnagaldur* must be inspired by that poem, which of course also emphasises the destruction of the earliest heathen gods. But in *Hrafnagaldur* the gods' powerlessness is accentuated by the fact that they can neither obtain knowledge for themselves about the future nor manage to find any counsel.

Besides having taken an interest in the art of ancient eddic poetry, which he learned about from Snorri's *Edda*, the poet also evidently knew the tradition of Latin epic. Hallgrímur Scheving argued convincingly (1837, 21) that Iðunn's shadowy life in the realm of death was inspired by Greco-Roman mythology (see, for example, Vergil's *Aeneid* VI, 390):

> því þó lýsingar þessar séu prýddar med ordatiltækjum úr nordurlandanna gudafrædi, þá er þó undirstadan og adferdin audsjáanliga løgud eptir þesskonar lýsingum rómverskra skálda, eda þeirra sem eptir þeim hafa stælt; því í gudakvædonum í Sæmundar eddu finnst ekkért þessháttar, en í hinum ødrum kvædaflokki Sæmundar eddu, minnist eg einasta þess fyrsta eyrindis í Hamþismálum, er álitist gæti sem eptirstæling rómversks skáldskapar.

One might also add that the long epic simile in stt. 13–14, too, must have been inspired by Greco-Roman poets. Scheving's conclusion was that the poem must be later than the other eddic poems, and that it must have been composed in the Christian period, which today seems a cautious one. Moreover, a further element in the poem that brings it still closer to Greco-Roman mythological narratives (e.g. the final scene of the *Iliad* Book I) than it is to Norse eddic poetry is the merry carousal that the gods indulge in, in spite of the awful events that are threatening. In the other eddic poems we nowhere see the gods seated together drinking merrily. In *Lokasenna*, where they are assembled for a drinking feast, the scene is not merry. The chariot of the sun in *Hrafnagaldur* is adorned with jewels, which leads one to think of Phoebus's chariot in Ovid's *Metamorphoses* (Book II 103). Finally, the description of Iðunn in *Hrafnagaldur* is also reminiscent of another passage in *Aeneid* VI (469–473), the account of the sorrow-stricken Dido in the world of the dead, where Aeneas speaks to her, but she does not answer, just looks down and turns away. Late in the seventeenth century, when Páll Vídalín was principal at the school of Skálholt, he was renowned for knowing the first six books of *The Aeneid* by heart (Jón Ólafsson úr Grunnavík 1950, 102).[21]

The poem distinguishes itself from the other eddic poems in that they give information about and names of things, places or figures in the Norse mythological world, which *Hrafnagaldur* does not do. The eddic poems are often allusive, but *Hrafnagaldur* contains obscure expressions to an exceptional degree. It uses names, words and kennings that otherwise seldom appear, either in eddic poetry or elsewhere. It is also the case that the syntax is reminiscent much more of skaldic poems or *rímur* than eddic poems.[22] This style, peculiar for an eddic poem, is certainly the reason that the poem has among scholars the reputation of being particularly obscure and extraordinary. The artificial syntax and the many kennings make it probable that the poet was more conversant with skaldic poetry and maybe especially *rímur* than with eddic poetry. Most of the figures or places from the Norse mythological world that are used in kennings in *Hrafnagaldur* are mentioned in Snorri's *Edda*, as is shown in the notes to the text below. Moreover, there is a number of names in *Hrafnagaldur* that are otherwise only known from Snorri's *Edda* or later texts. These are: 1) Niflheimr, 2) Døkkálfar, 3) Bifrǫst (only in the form *Bilrǫst* in eddic poems), 4) Jóln/ Jólnar (apparently only recorded in Snorri's *Edda* and a stanza (16 or 13) of *Háleygjatal* that is only transmitted in manuscripts of Snorri's *Edda*), 5) Nál, 6) Vingólf, 7) Hangatýr. In addition, there is the noun 'díar', which is

[21] Some of the syntax of *Hrafnagaldur*, such as the frequent asyndeton, the several examples of omission of a subject pronoun, and the rather frequent use of the dative case in place of a prepositional phrase (e.g. st. 19 'minnishornum', st. 23 'Hrímfaxa', st. 26 'Gjǫll'), is reminiscent of Latin.

[22] The metre generally seems to be a mistaken attempt to follow Old Norse patterns, analogously to the mistaken attempts at archaic word forms. The examples of prepositions in stressed position at the end of a line immediately followed by the word they govern at the beginning of the next line (stt. 5/5, 6/3, 7/3, 5) show a poor grasp of the rules of Old Norse prosody. Postpositions, on the other hand, are found in stressed position (*Hrafnagaldur* st. 10/6) quite commonly, cf. *Vǫluspá* 38/3, *Hávamál* 38/2, *Grímnismál* 21/3, 22/2, *Lokasenna* 24/2. Prepositions separated from the word they govern by other words are, however, occasionally found in stressed position in eddic poems, cf. *Vǫluspá* 26/5.

The lines consist preponderantly of Sievers's type A, and regularly with four syllables only, which gives them more the flavour of *rímur* patterns than those of eddic poetry; light lines such as st. 1/3 are not found in medieval *fornyrðislag*. St. 15/5 (′ x x ′) is anomalous. Type E should have a half stress between the two stresses. (On Sievers's five metrical types see his *Altgermanische Metrik*, 1893.) On the pattern of st. 1, cf. *Háttatal* 9; on that of st. 11/5–8, cf. the Third Grammatical Treatise, *SnE* 1848–1887, II 222–226 ('Antiteton', species 3 and 4).

found in both Snorri's *Edda* and *Heimskringla*, and finally 'man(n)heim(a)r', which is only recorded in *Ynglinga saga* in *Heimskringla*. The number of names and forms of names that are only known from Snorri's *Edda* shows that the poet must have known this work extremely well, and also the poem is really downright incomprehensible without the use of Snorri's *Edda* as a reference book while it is read. The poet may have used it as a handbook while he was writing. If it was composed under such circumstances, this would explain the poem's antiquarian and learned character and the high incidence of kennings. Snorri's *Edda* quotes only fragments of eddic poems in *Gylfaginning* in connection with narratives about gods and the mythological world. Just a couple of eddic poems are transmitted in a more or less complete form in manuscripts of Snorri's *Edda* (*Grottasǫngr* in the Codex Regius and *Rígsþula* in Codex Wormianus). Of most of the eddic poems he quotes such as *Vǫluspá* and *Grímnismál*, Snorri quotes single stanzas or a few consecutive stanzas.

Several eddic poems are a form of wisdom poetry. In the poems where the gods lack knowledge, *Baldrs draumar* and *Vǫluspá*, Óðinn sets out to procure it, in *Hyndluljóð* it is Freyja that sets out. *Hrafnagaldur* is also a wisdom poem, but it turns upside down some of the conventions that wisdom poems otherwise conform to. Óðinn does not himself set out, but sends other gods, and they do not get answers to their questions. But a search for an 'original' myth is unlikely ever to be fruitful, for the poet had scarcely any greater knowledge of Norse mythology than he was able to get out of reading Snorri's *Edda*. If the poem is an antiquarian product, composed with the help of Snorri's *Edda* by a learned person who was proud of and interested in the Icelanders' ancient poetic art, this would also explain why the content of the poem is not in keeping with the mythological stories that we now have from the Middle Ages. The poet may have got information from Snorri's *Edda* about kennings and mythological figures, and from this constructed his own narrative about Iðunn and the gods. The poem should not, however, be seen as a falsification, rather it should be seen as an expression of an antiquarian interest in the ancient eddic art. In the first printed writings about Iceland, learned Icelanders express pride in this art.

MANUSCRIPT TRANSMISSION

Hrafnagaldur is transmitted in at least thirty-seven copies. One manuscript (KB Add 14 4to) contains just a Latin translation, AM 424 fol. contains a commentary by Gunnar Pálsson. The manuscripts are found in Iceland, (Landsbókasafnið), Denmark (Det kongelige Bibliotek), Sweden (Kungliga biblioteket in Stockholm and Universitetsbiblioteket in Uppsala), Great

Britain (British Library in London, English Faculty Library in Oxford and National Library of Scotland in Edinburgh), Germany (Staatsbibliothek zu Berlin, Preussischer Kulturbesitz) and the USA (Harvard University Library). In addition, in Den Arnamagnæanske Samling in Copenhagen there is Gunnar Pálsson's commentary on the poem (in AM 424 fol.), which was used by Guðmundur Magnússon in *Edda* 1787–1828, I. The manuscripts in question are these:

Kungliga biblioteket, Stockholm:
 Stockholm papp. fol. nr 34 (34)
 Stockholm papp. fol. nr 57 (C)
 Stockholm papp. 4to nr 11 (11)
 Stockholm papp. 4to nr 46 (46)
 Stockholm papp. 8vo nr 15 (A)

Uppsala Universitetsbibliotek:
 UUB R 682 (682)
 UUB R 682 a (682 a)
 UUB R 691 (691)

Det kongelige Bibliotek, København:
 NKS 1108 fol. (1108)
 NKS 1109 fol. (1109)
 NKS 1111 fol. (1111)
 NKS 1866 4to (1866)
 NKS 1870 4to (1870)
 Thott 773 a fol. (773 a)
 Thott 1491 4to (D)
 Thott 1492 4to (1492)
 KB Add 14 4to (14)

Den Arnamagnæanske Samling, København:
 AM 424 fol.

Landsbókasafn Íslands, Háskólabókasafn, Reykjavík:
 Lbs 818 4to (818)
 Lbs 966 4to (966)
 Lbs 1441 4to (E)
 Lbs 1562 4to (B)
 Lbs 1588 a 4to (1588 a I and II)
 Lbs 1689 4to (1689)
 Lbs 2859 4to (2859)
 ÍBR 36 4to (36)
 ÍBR 24 8vo (24)

JS 648 4to (648)
JS 494 8vo (494)

British Library, London:
Add. 4877 (4877)
Add. 11165 (11165)
Egerton 643 (643)

National Library of Scotland, Edinburgh:
Adv. 21.4.7 (21.4.7)
Adv. 21.5.2 (21.5.2)
Adv. 21.6.7 (21.6.7)

English Faculty Library, Oxford:
ZCJ22 (22)

Staatsbibliothek zu Berlin, Preussischer Kulturbesitz:
Ms. germ. qu. 329 (329)

Harvard University Library, Harvard:
Ms. Icel. 47 (47)

The earliest manuscripts that contain the poem are A and B. Both were written in the second half of the seventeenth century. A was taken to Sweden by Guðmundur Ólafsson (c. 1652–1695) in 1681. B includes *Hrafnagaldur* and a few other eddic poems in the hand of Ásgeir Jónsson (c. 1657–1707).

It will be shown below that we can reckon with five manuscripts that have independent textual value, A, B, C, D and E. There are other manuscripts derived from A and B, but none, as far as is known, from C, D or E.

As already stated, the poem is only transmitted in a single version. The number and ordering of stanzas is the same in all manuscripts (though stt. 21 and 25 have been merged together in E), no manuscripts have any stanzas added or omitted, and there are only minor differences in the texts they contain. Variant readings are often just a case of words being joined together or not, or confusion of combinations of i, u, n, and m. The poem is composed in *fornyrðislag* in eight-line stanzas, and is written out in stanzas of 8 lines in most manuscripts (including D and E), though in A and B each stanza is written out as a single paragraph of prose covering about three lines and in C each pair of lines is written side by side, giving stanzas of four 'long' lines.

DESCRIPTION OF THE MANUSCRIPTS IN GROUP A

The A group consists of Stockholm papp. 8vo nr 15 and manuscripts derived from it. These copies reproduce the distinctive readings of A.

Stockholm papp. 8vo nr 15 (A)
The manuscript, which consists of 124 leaves, was written in the second half of the seventeenth century using both Gothic and cursive script. It is bound in a leaf from an antiphonary from c. 1300. It contains eddic poems in the following order: *Sólarljóð, Hrafnagaldur* (ff. 8r–10r; pp. 15–19), *Vǫluspá, Hávamál, Vafþrúðnismál, Grímnismál, Alvíssmál, Lokasenna, Þrymskviða, Hárbarðsljóð, Skírnismál, Hymiskviða* and *Baldrs draumar*. Then follow *Vǫlundarkviða* and the rest of the poems in the Codex Regius in the same order as in that manuscript, and after that *Fjölsvinnsmál, Hyndluljóð, Gróugaldur* and *Grottasǫngr*. Stanza numbers are added in the margin.

A is, as stated above, one of the earliest manuscripts that contain *Hrafnagaldur*. It is not known precisely when, where or by whom it was written but it was brought to Sweden in 1681 by Guðmundur Ólafsson (1652–1695) who, as mentioned in note 7 above, probably acquired it in Skálholt while he was studying there. It appears in Guðmundur's own register of the Icelandic manuscripts and books that he sold to Antikvitetskollegiet in 1684. There it is described as 'Sæmundar Edda, in 8:vo' (Gödel 1897, 179; cf. also Schück 1933, 98). Guðmundur, according to Gödel, made notes in various places in the margins of the manuscript. But notes are made in the margin in two different kinds of writing, Gothic style and cursive, which may be by two different hands. One of them (with Gothic style script) which among other things added variant readings or corrections in the margin by *Hrafnagaldur*, is, as far as one can judge, identical with the hand that wrote the text. On the flyleaf stands the name 'Johannes {Diethericus / Theodericus} Gröner', according to Gödel 'written, it appears, by the same ornate hand that executed the whole manuscript, and from whom also papp 8:vo nr 3 and 18 derive' (Gödel 1897–1900, 376), but there seems to be no foundation for this identification. 'Johannes {Diethericus / Theodericus} Gröner' is presumably the Danish diplomat Johan Diderik Grüner (1661–1712). For a time he resided with the polymath Ole Borch (1626–1690), who belonged to the circle of Ole Worm and Thomas Bartholin the Elder. In 1683 Grüner accompanied a relative of Borch to Stockholm, where from 1688 to 1698 he was secretary to the Danish embassy under Bolle Christensen Luxdorph (1643–1698). Borch may have aroused an interest in antiquities in Grüner, who could have borrowed the manuscript from him and written his name in it.

There are the following distinctive readings in A:

st. 15: ad þeckia f*yrir* A] at syn v*ar fyrir* B, at syn var fyrer C, at syn var fyrir D, ad syn var fyrir E

st. 16: Grymis A] Gr*i*mnis B, grun*n*is C, Grimnis D, Grimnis E

st. 24: rokna A] jarkna B, C, jarkna D, iarkna E
st. 25: jadyr A] jodyr B, C, jo dyr D, iodyr E

These four distinctive readings in A are secondary, since they are probably cases of definite errors that came about in the copying. In st. 15, 'þeckia' is added in the margin in A by the same hand that wrote the poem, possibly because the scribe had accidentally omitted the word, and it is probably an error or a bad guess. This couplet had no alliteration in A: 'sokte þvi meir | ad þeckia fyrer', whereas it does in B, C, D and E ('soktu/sokto þvi meir | ad syn var fyrir'). In st. 24, the scribe of A has written 'jokna' in the margin by 'rokna', indicating that he knew there was something wrong in what he had written in the text.

Two readings on the other hand are in all likelihood primary:

st. 7: hardbaþms A] hardbaþins B, hardbaþnis C, harþbaþnis D, harbadms E
st. 22: Omi A] Onn B, On*n* C, Oþinn D, Ome E

The two readings 'hardbaþms' and 'Omi' must be regarded as superior to the readings of the other manuscripts in these places. 'Oþinn' (in D) is certainly better, but A's 'Omi' may be preferred on the principle of *lectio difficilior potior*. This reading is also supported by E. 'Onn' in B and C must be due to a misreading of the four minims in 'Omi', like the readings of A and C for 'Grímnis' in st. 16, and 'Oþinn' could be due to a scribe's assumption that 'Onn' was an abbreviation for that name lacking the usual superior stroke. It is more difficult to explain how 'Omi' and 'Onn' could be derived from an original 'Oþinn'.

Rask compares A with his text in his edition of the *Edda* (Stockholm 1818), though he mistakenly refers to it as nr 5, and variants from A are given to the text of *Hrafnagaldur*, where it is given the siglum F. Bugge, in his edition of the *Edda* compared the text in A, which he refers to as St., with the Codex Regius, but his edition of *Hrafnagaldur* is not based on A, and he does not give variants from it (*Norrœn fornkvæði* 1867, xlviii; xlix; liii–lv). Finally, Barend Sijmons used A in *Die Lieder der Edda* (Halle 1888–1906), but did not, however, include *Hrafnagaldur*. A was most recently used by Jónas Kristjánsson when he published its text of *Hrafnagaldur* in *Morgunblaðið* (2002).

The text of *Hrafnagaldur* is here based on that of A, which has fewer errors than the other manuscripts.

The following manuscripts are direct or indirect copies of A:

Stockholm papp. fol. nr 34 (34)
This manuscript, which consists of 506 leaves, was written in 1684. It is half-bound in leather, and contains both Snorri's *Edda* (ff. 1–284) and

eddic poems (ff. 285–506) in the same order as in A. The eddic poems, including *Hrafnagaldur*, are arranged in two columns with the Icelandic text parallel to a Latin translation.

According to Gödel (1897–1900, 144), the Icelandic text of the eddic poems in this manuscript was copied from A in Stockholm in 1684 by Helgi Ólafsson (c. 1646–1707), Guðmundur Ólafsson's brother. In the text of *Hrafnagaldur* all the innovations of A are reproduced. The translation of the first thirteen stanzas of *Hrafnagaldur* was also carried out by Helgi, but then another translator took over. Helgi worked as amanuensis at Antikvitetskollegiet from 1682 to 1686 with a break in 1683, when he went to visit his family in Iceland (Gödel 1897, 188). On the last leaf is written: 'Finitum Holmiæ in posterioris idib*us* Maij Anno 1684. Helgus Olaus islandus'.

The part of the manuscript containing eddic poems was used in Guðmundur Magnússon's edition (*Edda* 1787–1828, I xliv), by Rask (*Edda Sæmundar hinns fróda* 1818) and by Bugge in establishing a *terminus ante quem* for A (*Norræn fornkvæði* 1867, liii).

NKS 1870 4to (1870)

This manuscript, which consists of 162 leaves, was written towards the end of the seventeenth century and bound in leather. Ff. 18v and 24v are blank, f. 104 is an inserted slip. It is mainly written in cursive on folded sheets and in a single hand, in a part of the manuscript in two columns, Icelandic text with parallel Latin translation. In a few cases notes are added at the side of stanzas in a different ink, but in the same hand. The manuscript bears the title 'Sæmundar Edda'. On f. 1v a list of contents is added and some remarks. Besides the eddic poems the manuscript contains three passages with the headings 'Hvad Gräkerne och annat Folk tagit ur wåra Norska fäders aldra äldsta Skriffter. Om Gyllende Tahlet. Himmelens Tecken', which are written in a different hand and inserted between *Brot af Sigurðarkviðu* and *Guðrúnarkviða I* on ff. 91v–100, and also some extracts from Resen's Latin preface to Guðmundur Andrésson's *Lexicon Islandicum* (Havniæ 1683) on ff. 161–162.

The eddic poems appear in the same order as in A. *Hrafnagaldur* comes on ff. 9r–11v. After *Hrafnagaldur* the title of *Vǫluspá* is written, but the poem itself is missing. At the end of *Grottasǫngr* (f. 160v) is written, as in 34: 'Finitum Holmiæ in posteriorib. Idib. Maj a. 1684 Helgus Olai isl.' The eddic poems, including *Hrafnagaldur*, are copied from 34 (there are a few errors in the text of *Hrafnagaldur,* for example st. 8: 'syria', where 34 has 'syrgia'), as is the Latin translation, in which only just a few alterations have been made in *Hrafnagaldur* (especially in stt. 24 and 25).

The manuscript seems to have been written in Stockholm. It could have been acquired and brought to Denmark by Johan Diderik Grüner in 1698. Variants from 1870 are quoted (with the siglum 'Svec.') to the text of *Hrafnagaldur* in the Arnamagnæan edition of the eddic poems (*Edda* 1787–1828, I) via Jón Eiríksson's manuscript, denoted 'E', which had been in Suhm's collection as no. 393 4to (see under 47 below), in which Jón had included variants from 1870.

UUB R 691 (691)

This manuscript, which consists of 49 leaves, was written in the eighteenth century in a single hand. It contains no information about when or by whom it was written, but on the inside of the front cover it states that it had belonged in Nordin's collection ('Uppsala Universitets Bibliothek. Nordins Saml. 220'). According to Gödel's catalogue it came into the Uppsala library in 1814 with that collection. It is half-bound in leather and reads on the spine: 'CARMINA ISLANDICA'. Several poems are written in two columns, Icelandic text with Latin translation parallel. According to Gödel's catalogue, the manuscript is a copy of 34, which must be right, for corrections are included in brackets within the lines of the stanzas in the same way as they are in 34. 691, however, has some of the poems in a different order (*Þrymskviða*, *Skírnismál*, *Baldrs draumar*, *Vǫlundarkviða*, *Rúnatal* in *Hávamál* (i.e. stt. 138 onwards), *Vafþrúðnismál*, *Grímnismál*, *Alvíssmál*, *Lokasenna*, *Hrafnagaldur* (ff. 39r–41v), *Sólarljóð*). It can also be said to be the same translation as in 34, though not all the possible alternative translations given in 34 are included, and moreover a few changes have been made. 691 also has certain innovations: in st. 15 it has the reading 'jolmin' for 34's 'Jölnum'. This turns up again in 1870, also a copy of 34.

UUB R 682 (682)

This manuscript, which consists of 83 leaves, was written in the eighteenth century in a single hand. F. 12v is blank. It is half-bound in leather and reads on the spine: 'EDDA SÆMUNDI PARTES XI'. The text in many places is written in two columns, Icelandic text with Latin translation parallel. The manuscript includes Latin translations of *Sólarljóð*, *Hrafnagaldur*, *Rúnatal* in *Hávamál*, *Vafþrúðnismál*, *Grímnismál*, *Alvíssmál*, *Lokasenna*, *Þrymskviða*, *Hárbarðsljóð* and *Skírnismál*. Its history is unknown, and there is no information about when it came into Uppsala Universitetsbibliotek, nor any in the manuscript about when or by whom it was written. It is marked N:o 619 (f. 1v) and once belonged to the same collection as UUB R 684 (cf. Gödel 1892, 27, 30), a copy of

Snorri's *Edda* made by Eric of Sotberg (1724–1781), who was secretary to Vitterhets-Akademien.

According to Gödel's catalogue, 682 is a copy of 34, which must be right. It has the poems in the same order as 34 (*Sólarljóð, Hrafnagaldur* (f. 9r–12r), *Vǫluspá, Hávamál, Vafþrúðnismál, Grímnismál, Alvíssmál, Lokasenna, Þrymskviða, Hárbarðsljóð, Skírnismál*, but it includes only the first eleven of the poems in 34 and A, cf. the title on the spine. It has the same corrections as 34, written out in the same way, either in brackets within the stanza or in brackets immediately at the end of the line.[23] The Latin text in 682 is also a copy of that in 34. Just a very few of the possible alternative translations given in 34 are omitted.

Stockholm papp. 4to nr 46 (46)

This manuscript, which consists of 138 leaves, was written in the latter part of the seventeenth century, but before 1690, and its text is arranged in two columns. It was half-bound in leather, according to information on the flyleaf in the year 1842, and the title on the spine is 'SÆMUNDAR-EDDA'.

46 is a copy of A in Guðmundur Ólafsson's hand. It has the poems in the same order as in A. *Hrafnagaldur* is written on pp. 13–17. Corrections that are added in the margin in A are in a few places inserted within the stanza in 46. In st. 24 it has 'jokna' within the stanza and 'rokna' in the margin. The innovations of A appear in 46, but 46 has secondary readings and corrections compared with A, e.g. st. 13, 'hvǫrri', and an instance of misreadings of minims, st. 15, 'jŏlmun'. The secondary readings in 46 also appear in the manuscript written by Gabriel Duhre (11), which therefore must have been copied from 46 and not from A; they also appear in 682 a. Besides, Duhre himself says in his copy that it was taken from Guðmundur Ólafsson's manuscript. 682 a is also a copy of 46.

46 was used in Rask's *Edda* (1818).

Stockholm papp. 4to nr 11 (11)

This manuscript, which consists of 208 leaves, was written in 1690 by Gabriel Duhre. It is half-bound in leather and reads on the spine: 'SÆMUNDAR-EDDA'. *Hrafnagaldur* is written in two columns, but the Latin translation that follows is written in a single column.

The manuscript contains the same poems as A and in the same order. Gödel says in his catalogue (1897–1900, 274) that it is a copy of A, but this is wrong. It is, as stated above, a copy of 46. Moreover at the end of the manuscript Duhre has written: 'Endir Sæmundar eddu. D. 19 Aprilis

---

[23] In st. 24 the scribe of 682 wrote '(:Jokna:)' within the stanza, whereas this reading is given beside the line in 34.

A:o 1690 Lycktade iag dänna Sæmunders Edda, som effter Jsländarens Gudmunn Olssons ägit manuscript, som war reent wackert och läsligt, hafwer iag nu till mitt ägit behof afskrifwit. Gabriel Duhre'.

11, unlike A, gives no variant readings or corrections in the margins, but some of the corrections that are placed in the margin in A are here incorporated into the text (st. 15, 'þeckia', st. 23, 'Jarþar', st. 24, 'Jokna' and st. 26, 'Niflheim'), but one correction or variant is omitted (st. 25, 'neþra'). 11 also contains the same Latin translation as 34, apart from sometimes, where 34 gives possible alternative translations, giving only one of the alternatives.

Bugge mentions this manuscript in *Norrœn fornkvæði* (1867, liii), but says he has not seen it himself.

UUB R 682 a (682 a)

This manuscript, which consists of 479 leaves, was written in the eighteenth century. It is bound in paper and reads on the spine: 'R. 682: a / Edda Sæmundar ins fröþa.' On f. 1r the title of the manuscript is given as 'EDDA | Sæmundar | ins | fröþa.' F. 1v is blank, but on f. 2r begins a list of contents, 'Innehalld bőkarennar'. The book contains the eddic poems in the same order as in A. There is no information in the manuscript about when or by whom it was written. Additions to *Hrafnagaldur* are written in the margins in the same ink and in the same cursive hand as the poem itself.

682 a seems to be a copy of 46, since it has innovations compared with A in common with 46. 682 a has probably, however, had further corrections added in the margins beyond those in its original (e.g. st. 1, 'þursar', st. 2, 'viltu', st. 4, 'ofan'). Only 46 and 682 a write in st. 5 the line 'vitiþ enn? eþa hvaþ?' with two question marks. They also both give the reading 'Loftur' in the margin by st. 9. These two manuscripts are besides the only manuscripts in the A group that have 'jokna' in the text of st. 24 and 'rokna' as a variant. In the other manuscripts it is the other way round.

In 1904 this manuscript, together with other books and manuscripts, was handed over for safe keeping at Uppsala Universitetsbibliotek by Kungliga Vetenskapssocieteten.

The following stemma of the manuscripts in the A group can be drawn up:

		A		
	46		34	
11	682 a	1870	691	682

Introduction

DESCRIPTION OF THE MANUSCRIPTS IN GROUP B

The B group consists of Lbs 1562 4to (B) and manuscripts derived from it. These copies reproduce the distinctive readings of B.

Lbs 1562 4to (B)
This manuscript, which has 148 leaves, was, according to Páll Eggert Ólason's catalogue, written c. 1660 and in the eighteenth century. (The date of 1660 must relate to the parts written by Ásgeir Jónsson, who was born c. 1657, and is too early. His part in the writing of the manuscript must have been done while he was studying in Skálholt, from 1673 to 1677.) It is in poor condition and has in several places crumbled away so that all that is left is the middle part of some of the original pages. It comprises a collection of gatherings and loose leaves that originally belonged to different manuscripts. In its present state it seems to be written in eight or nine hands.

The manuscript contains mainly eddic poems. It opens on f. 2r with 'Registur ifer þessa Sæmundar | Eddu', which must be a list of contents to a manuscript of which only fragments now survive in B. It is this part of the existing manuscript that is of interest in connection with *Hrafnagaldur.* According to the list of contents it had the poems in the following order: *Sólarljóð, Hrafnagaldur, Vǫluspá, Hávamál, Vafþrúðnismál, Grímnismál, Skírnismál, Hárbárðsljóð, Lokasenna, Þrymskviða, Baldrs draumar, Vǫlundarkviða*, after which the heroic poems follow in their usual order up to and including *Hamðismál*. Then come these poems: *Fjölsvinnsmál, Hyndluljóð, Gróugaldur, Grottasǫngr* and *Heiðreks gátur*. At the end of the list it says: 'Getspeki Heiðreks kongs vantar mig aldeilis i báda codices'. *Heiðreks gátur* now follows the list of contents and is in the same eighteenth-century hand, but these items must have been added at a later stage, long after the original manuscript that the list relates to had been written; 'báda codices' presumably relates to Ásgeir Jónsson's manuscript and one of the others from which B is now compiled.

The list of contents probably relates to a collection of eddic poems written by Ásgeir Jónsson of which only the following items now survive in B: *Sólarljóð*, which is fragmentary (ff. 7r–11v) and *Hrafnagaldur* (ff. 12r–13v and 16r; these two poems follow immediately after *Heiðreks gátur*); and *Atlamál* (stt. 41/8–65/5 on ff. 14 and 15, which are attached to each other, and are in the wrong place, in the middle of *Hrafnagaldur*, and the rest on ff. 131r–136v) and *Baldrs draumar* (ff. 141r–142r).

The rest of the existing manuscript did not belong to this collection of eddic poems, and is in various seventeenth or eighteenth-century hands. The manuscript as we have it has altogether the following items: Contents,

Heiðreks gátur (both written in the same hand), *Sólarljóð*, *Hrafnagaldur* (both written in Ásgeir's hand), brief notes and summary extracts from *Laufás Edda* (written in a third hand), *Vǫluspá* and *Hávamál* to st. 63 (in a fourth hand), more from *Laufás Edda* (these leaves seem to have been inserted later, and are perhaps in a fifth hand, though it is very similar to the third; there are here also some 'Variantes lectiones' in a different ink and almost certainly a different hand), continuation of *Hávamál* (to st. 110) (again in the fourth hand), extracts from *Laufás Edda* continued (one leaf in the fifth hand), continuation of *Hávamál* (to st. 127), extracts from *Laufás Edda* continued (two leaves in the fifth hand), the rest of *Hávamál* and *Vafþrúðnismál* to *Brot af Sigurðarkviðu* in the order of the Codex Regius, again in the fourth hand; then in a new, sixth hand, beginning on a new leaf, the final stanzas of *Guðrúnarkviða I*, *Sigurðarkviða in skamma*, *Helreið Brynhildar* (in this poem, the fourth hand resumes), *Guðrúnarkviða II*, *Guðrúnarkviða III*, *Oddrúnargrátr*, *Atlakviða*, *Guðrúnarhvǫt*, *Hamðismál*. Then in a new (seventh) hand, passages from *Vǫlsunga saga* to cover the lacuna of the Codex Regius; *Atlamál* in Ásgeir's hand; *Fjölsvinnsmál*, *Hyndluljóð*, *Grottasǫngr* in a new hand (probably identical with the sixth hand); *Baldrs draumar* in Ásgeir's hand; and finally, in a further new hand, 'Evrópa', a piece of writing about Europe and Asia.

In the list of contents for the original manuscript that contained *Hrafnagaldur*, on f. 2r by the name *Hávamál*, has been added:

> I midium Havamalu*m* 2 erendum fyr enn biriar / Ræd eg þer / lodfafnir / – hefur S*íra* Helge sem var ã stad skrifad þa ha*nn* var i stock holm. Annar partur Lod fafnis liod. qvod noto si forte sveci ita vocent aut citent caput aliqvod Sæmundar eddu. Vix aliud Mysterium suberit.

This is the first of a number of references to Helgi in the list of contents, which may be why it is the most detailed of them. They imply that Helgi Ólafsson, Guðmundur Ólafsson's brother, had made notes against the texts of some of the poems in the original manuscript while he was in Stockholm in the years 1682 to 1686 (cf. the account of 34). B has thus, like A, been in Sweden in the hands of the brothers Guðmundur and Helgi Ólafsson at some time. There is nothing, however, to indicate that the manuscript itself was written in Sweden; it rather originates in Skálholt (see footnote 7 above).

It is known that Páll Vídalín owned some eddic poems that had been written by Ásgeir Jónsson and Helgi Ólafsson (Jón Helgason 1926, 287, note), and these were probably identical with the surviving eddic poems in B in Ásgeir's hand (cf. the account of 1588 a below). Ásgeir was tutor in Vídalín's home in 1716 to 1717, and it is conceivable that he brought his manuscript there with him. In a list of manuscripts and books in Páll's possession made by Jón Ólafsson of Grunnavík (Add. 11245, preserved in the British Library), a manuscript is mentioned that could be identical with this part of B: 'onnur [i.e. Sæmundar Edda] med hende Sr Helga og ymsra. fyrst ä henne Sölarliöd Sæm(undar) fröda og Hrafnag(aldur) Odins med hendi Øgm(undar) Ogm(unds)s(onar)'. *Hrafnagaldur* in B was not written by Ögmundur Ögmundarson (died 1707), but Jón's attribution to him could be a mistake, for he wrote his catalogue of Vídalín's library from memory in about 1730, some years after he had gone to Copenhagen (Jón Helgason 1985, 16, 20, 29).

Giovanni Verri has identified the hand that wrote *Hrafnagaldur* in B as Ásgeir Jónsson's, since it uses his characteristic 'vellum-like' cursive (2007, 23). According to Agnete Loth (1960, 212) it is possible that Ásgeir Jónsson used this script in his earliest period of copying in the 1680s when copying parchment manuscripts, though this theory has since been contested by Hubert Seelow (1977).

Each stanza of *Hrafnagaldur* in B is written as a paragraph of prose in the same way as in A, but in contrast to that manuscript, here the stanzas are not numbered. The following distinctive readings are found in B:

st. 1: normr B] nornir A, C, D, E
st. 3: þur B] þvi A, C, D, E
st. 3: Þrains B] Þranis A, D Þrãnis C, Þraens E
st. 7: hardbaþins B] hardbaþms A, hardbaþnis C, harþbaþnis D, harbadms E
st. 7: miðir B] undir A, C, D, under E
st. 9: sumni B] sunnu A, E, sun*n*o C, sunno D
st. 13: ofǫnþg*ar*ð B] of miþgard A, C, of miþgarþ D, of midgard E
st. 19: Mimis B] min*n*is A, C, minnis D, minnes E
st. 23: mosar B] moþir A, C, moþr D, moder E
st. 26: Ulfrimar B] Ulfrunar A, C, D, E

Most of the distinctive readings in B are obviously corrupt and must be scribal errors that arose in copying. 'Mimis', however, is not necessarily an error. But all the other manuscripts have 'minnis/minnes' here, which is surely correct, since in the context it is more meaningful to speak of 'minnishorn' ('toast-horns') than 'Mímis horn' ('Mímir's horns'). This and the variants in stt. 1, 7, 9, 26 are moreover nearly all the result of misreading of minims, and have little if any significance. On the other hand 'Þrains' in st. 3 is obviously the correct reading (it is confirmed by E); in this case it is the scribes of the other manuscripts that have misread the minims, unless 'Þranis' was in the archetype and it was corrected by the scribes of B and E from their knowledge of mythology.

The majority of the preserved texts of *Hrafnagaldur* are derived directly or indirectly from B. These manuscripts are as follows.

Lbs 966 4to (966)

This manuscript consists of 154 leaves and according to Páll Eggert Ólason's *Skrá um Handritasöfn Landsbókasafnsins*, was written by three hands in the second half of the eighteenth century. Ff. 92–94, 117r, 141v, 148v–149 and 152v are blank. The existing manuscript, which is unbound, contains eddic poems, other pre-Reformation poems and legal texts.

On a loose leaf several names are written, of which some are illegible. The following can be made out: 'Welæruverðugum heiðursmanni | Siera Einari Ólafsine | Jón Gíslason Steinhólm | Gisle Jonsson Steinholm | Jon Gislason Steinholm | a þessa bok | Olafur Jonsson | Gísli Jónsson | Narfi Einarsson'. On the back of this leaf is written the end of a letter with the signature of Ólafur Einarsson and the date 'di 22 Februarii 1798'. On a piece of paper stored with 966 that has probably been used for binding is written 'Steinhólmsbók', a name for the book which must have originated with its owners.

According to Páll Eggert Ólason the manuscript was bought by Björn M. Ólsen in 1904. On a leaf stored with the manuscript Ólsen has written the following notes:

> Bókina hefir átt Guðrún Jónsdóttir. Jón faðir hennar var Gíslason og kallaði sig Steinhólm, af því að hann hafði alizt upp á Steinanesi í Arnarfirði. Þessi Jón átti 3 börn, Guðrúnu, Gísla föður Þuríðar á Núpi og Guðrúnu, sem bókina átti. Jón var ættaður að norðan. Guðrún þessi var gipt Brynjólfi Brynjólfssyni, sem bjó að Núpi í Dýrafirði.
>
> Handritið af Sólarljóðum sýnist vera skyldast hddr. Cx og Lx hjá Bugge.
>
> 1853 á bókina Brynjólfur Brynjólfsson á Núpi við Dýrafjörð (eftir áskrift á Bókinni sjálfri). (bl. 112).

Bugge's manuscripts Cx and Lx that are mentioned by Ólsen are 1866 and 1109. As far as *Hrafnagaldur* is concerned, 1109 is more closely related to 966 than either 1108, which was also used by Bugge in his edition, or 1866 is.

The first two gatherings of 966 contain pre-Reformation religious poems. The third contains *Sólarljóð*, *Hrafnagaldur* (ff. 21v–23v), *Baldrs draumar* and *Grottasǫngr*. This last poem, we are told, was 'Ritaðr eptir Bók Páls Sveinssonar Torfasonar, en su bók med hendi Sira Jóns sem var i Villingaholti' (f. 25v). Then follow *Gróugaldr*, *Fjölsvinnsmál*, *Hyndluljóð*, *Hávamál*, royal decrees, Snorri Sturluson's genealogy, a chronological table from the birth of Óðinn down to the year 1000, Ólafur Jónsson of Purkey's genealogy, a collection of legal texts and decrees, Jón Bjarnason of Rafnseyri's genealogy (after which is added 'epter hanns eiginhandar Riti'), small sections of the genealogies of the Lund and Gilsbakki families and finally more decrees.

After the last of the eddic poems, *Hávamál*, there is a 'Forordning um*m* afgift af erfda gótze þan*n* 12 sept. 1792'. This heading is written in the same hand as the preceding poems, including *Hrafnagaldur*, so this part of the manuscript must have been written after that date. Its text of *Hrafnagaldur* reproduces the distinctive readings of B and could be a copy of B (cf. Verri 2007, 40–41). But in contrast to B, *Hrafnagaldur* is here arranged with each pair of verse lines written side by side so that eight verse lines cover four lines of writing, though the stanzas are unnumbered as in B. The error in stanza division in stt. 20–21 (see p. 13 above) is corrected. A number of innovations in comparison with B have been introduced: st. 1, 'okk*ar*', st. 13, 'of*o*nd*a*rgð', st. 15, 'korarnn', st. 18, 'vist', st. 20, 'himin', st. 26, 'himin'. In particular, the error 'korarnn' in st. 15 for 'kominn' suggests that 966 may be a direct copy of B, since the 'm' in B could at first glance be mistaken as 'ra'.

The manuscript is discussed by Jónas Kristjánsson (1967) in connection with *Gróugaldur* and *Fjölsvinnsmál*.

A certain number of manuscripts within the B group (1109, 1492, 773 a, 1866, 47, 21.4.7, 4877, 22, 1108, 11165) were derived from a manuscript (Jón Egilsson's manuscript) that had been collated with a now lost manuscript owned by Eyjólfur Jónsson (1670–1745), priest at Vellir in Svarfaðardalur and Gunnar Pálsson's tutor. In this sub-group variant readings have been entered in the margins. Since there are no variants to the text of *Hrafnagaldur* from Eyjólfur's manuscript in any manuscript of this subgroup, it may be that the poem was not included in Eyjólfur's manuscript. The manuscripts in this sub-group reproduce the distinctive readings of B, but also share innovations compared with B, for instance in st. 15, 'mar' (line 5) and 'Jorna' (line 1).

NKS 1109 fol. (1109)

This manuscript consists of 251 leaves plus a letter that is bound in with it at the beginning. It was written in the eighteenth century, has a leather binding with gold tooling embossed with Luxdorph's library mark (a gold elephant, though in the course of time it has turned black). On the spine the title 'Edda Sæmundi' is stamped and on the title page it reads 'Sæmundar Eddu [sic] | ens Froþa.| ɔ: | Edda Sæmundi.' The manuscript, which has irregular pagination, is written in a single hand. On the verso of the end flyleaf Luxdorph has written his name at the top left.

The letter at the beginning of the manuscript is dated November 1769 by vice lawman Jón Ólafsson of Eyri in Seyðisfjörður (1729–1778). He also informs us on a slip placed in the manuscript that it had belonged to Luxdorph and was derived from a manuscript belonging to Jón Egilsson (1714–1784), once vice-principal at Hólar and later priest at Laufás, that had been collated with a manuscript in Eyjólfur Jónsson's own hand:

Dette Hr. Conference-Raad B. W. Luxdorphi Exemplar af Edda Sæmundi in folio bestaaende af 34 kvidur eller odis . . . . de saa kaldte Sæmundar Lióð er en fast accurat og paalidelig Afskrift af den Edda, som forrige Con-Rector paa Holum John Egilsen, nu Pastor Laufasensis, har været Eyere af, hvilket Exemplar ikke alleene er bleven confereret med nogle Codicibus chartaceis og en gl. Membr. men og med en meget ypperlig Codice chart. egenhændig skreven af Sal. Hr. Ejulf Jonssen, fordum Præst til Walle udi Svarfaderdahl, en mand der i sin tiid var en af de lærdeste Islændere og berömt Antiqvarius. . . . November 1769. J. Olavssön Vice-Laugmand i Island.

It is stated as well in the letter that variants marked 'c.E.' came from Eyjólfur Jónsson's manuscript.

We are also told that the manuscript has variants from manuscripts on paper and vellum owned by Bjarni Halldórsson (1703–1773), sheriff at Þingeyrar. From a list of printed books and manuscripts left by Bjarni Halldórsson in NKS 1852 4to (printed in Jón Helgason 1985, 34–38), it can be seen that he had owned three so-called Sæmundar eddur. One of them may have been the manuscript that had previously been in the possession of Páll Vídalín and Jón Ólafsson of Grunnavík.[24] Bjarni Halldórsson, who had married into Páll Vídalín's family, was Jón Ólafsson's father-in-law. Bjarni Halldórsson's wife, Hólmfríður, was daughter of Páll Vídalín and Þorbjörg, daughter of Magnús Jónsson of Vigur (see Jón Helgason 1926, 287, note; 1985, 6–7, 34–37). In the surviving manuscript 1588 a there is preserved the list of contents of a Sæmundar Edda that has the initials 'B.H.S', which could be Bjarni Halldórsson (Verri 2007, 28), but the manuscript the list relates to has not been preserved (cf. the description of 1588 a).

The order of the poems is as in the Codex Regius, but *Baldrs draumar*, *Grottasǫngr*, *Gróugaldur*, *Fjölsvinnsmál* and *Hyndluljóð* have been inserted between *Þrymskviða* and *Vǫlundarkviða*. After *Hamðismál* follow *Hrafnagaldur* (pp. 452–460; ff. 226v–230v), *Heiðreks gátur* and *Sólarljóð*. 1109 thus has the poems in the same order as 1492 and 773 a. Its text ends at the same place in *Sólarljóð* as that in 773 a. The lacuna in the Codex Regius is filled from Eyjólfur Jónsson's manuscript ('Hæc ex cod. Dni. Ey.'), the variants marked 'c.E.' and 'al' are also found in 1492 and 773 a. The same possible corrections to the text of *Hrafnagaldur* are given in all three manu-

---

[24] This was probably B, and the same manuscript that Jón Ólafsson of Grunnavík tried to get hold of for Møllmann, royal historiographer and librarian at Det kongelige Bibliotek, when he wanted in 1755 to obtain a good copy of the eddic poems in connection with the Arnamagnæan Commission's plans to publish Snorri's Edda, but Bjarni Halldórsson would neither lend it nor allow it to be copied. Bjarni's possessiveness with this manuscript may be one of the reasons why the text of *Hrafnagaldur* is so poorly preserved in Icelandic manuscripts.

scripts, and st. 19, 'Ragna' and st. 24, 'mannheim' are stated to be 'forte'. 1109 reproduces some of the distinctive readings of B (for example st. 3, 'þur', 'Þrains', st. 9, 'sumni', st. 13, 'ond-garþ', st. 19, 'mimis', st. 23, 'mosar', st. 26, 'ulfrimar'). But it does not have all of them: it has 'nornir' in st. 1, where B has 'normr', and in st. 7, 'harþ-baþms undir', where B has 'hardbaþins miðir'. These two, however, only relate to errors in reading minims, which any scribe can make or correct independently. 1109 has a few innovations: st. 9, 'virir', st. 15, 'jotnum', 'mar', st. 21, 'syanna'. These appear in 1492 and 773 a too. All three have the error in stanza division in stt. 20 and 21. In 1109 *Hrafnagaldur* is arranged in unnumbered eight-line stanzas.

The manuscript was once in Suhm's collection, no. 877 fol. ('e bibl. Luxd.'). It was used by Bugge (*Norrœn fornkvæði* 1867, xlvi; xlix; lii; lx), where it has the siglum C. It is also mentioned in Jónas Kristjánsson 1987.

Thott 1492 4to (1492)

This manuscript, which has 162 leaves, was written in the eighteenth century and has never been bound. It contains a Sæmundar Edda. A slip inserted at the beginning gives the following information:

> Edda Sæmundar fróda ɔ: Edda Sæmundi Polihistoris cum contextis quarundam odarum et variantibus lectionibus collata cum codice Domini Eyulfi Pastoris prædii Vallensis in Islandia boreali /: Antiquitatum patriæ viri peritissimi :/ ex tribus aliis manuscriptis cartaceis et memb. Exemplar rarum, ubi in margine litteræ c.E. indicant codicem Eyulfi et littere al. denotant cartas. 2 Edda Snorronis impressa accuratior.

That is, the contents of this manuscript are very similar to those in 1109, including the variant readings from the same sources. The final phrase, that says it is more accurate than the printed edition of the second Edda, Snorri's, fits with the prevailing view of the time, that the collection of eddic poems was much more ancient than Snorri's work.

The order of the poems is the same as in 1109 and 773 a. *Hrafnagaldur* is written on ff. 146v–149r.

Variants marked 'c.E.' or 'al' are found throughout, but not to the text of *Hrafnagaldur*, though two alternative readings are given to the poem, 'Ragna', st. 19, and 'Mannheim', st. 24, both marked 'forte'. Like 1109, 1492 reproduces some of B's distinctive readings (e.g. st. 3, 'þur', 'Þrains', st. 9, 'sumni', st. 13, 'ǫnd-garþ', st. 19, 'mimis', st. 23, 'mosar', st. 26, 'ulfrimar'), but with the same exceptions as 1109. It also has the same innovations.

Thott 773 a fol. (773 a)

This manuscript, which consists of 230 leaves, was written in the eighteenth century. It is half-bound in leather, and has gold tooling on the spine, though most of it has now gone. It was restored by Birgitte Dall in 1976.

The content is eddic poems. It bears the title 'Sæmundar Edda ens fröþa'. On the recto of the flyleaf Thott has written: 'Vdskrefven efter Hr. Iohn Ejelfsen Præst paa Laafaas, hands Membrana, som holdes for at være megedt god'. At the bottom is added 'Kost. 10 rd.' On the inside of the front cover we read: 'Sa John Ejilfssen / Præst paa Laafaas'. This must be a mistake for the Jón Egilsson that was the owner of the manuscript from which 1109 and probably 1492 were derived.

773 a gives the same variants as 1492 and 1109, has the poems in the same order, and gives the same possible amendments to the text of *Hrafnagaldur*, which is written on pp. 424–430 (ff. 212r–215r), as 1492. It also reproduces the innovations common to 1109 and 1492. It is difficult to determine the relationships of 1492, 1109 and 773 a, since there are very few variant readings that they do not all three share. 1492 shares one error with 773 a that is not in 1109, st. 26, 'mola' for 'niola'. In 1109, 'ni' in 'niola' is clearly written, so it seems unlikely that the error can have arisen in a copy of it. 773 a has the same error as 1109 in st. 13, 'kinr', which is not in 1492. If 1109 was a copy of 773 a, and both were derived from 1492, the error 'kinr' could have arisen in 773 a, and that in 'mola' in 1492 as confusion in the reading of the minims in 'ni'; this obvious error might have been corrected by the scribe of 1109 from his knowledge of *Alvíssmál* or *Skáldskaparmál*.

NKS 1866 4to (1866)

This manuscript consists of 182 leaves irregularly paginated 1–357 (+ 3 preliminary leaves and 2 blank leaves just before the back cover). It is leather bound with Luxdorph's library mark, the gold elephant, and gold tooling on the spine, which bears the title: 'EDDA SÆMUNDI'. On f. 3r there is the heading: 'Edda | Sæmundar Pre|stz ins fröda Sigfuz|sonar at Odda | Skrifud a äre epter | Guds Burd | 1750'. On f. 2v Luxdorph has written his name. The title page is very elaborately executed, and at the bottom is added 'Pinxit HKS'. It has not been possible to identify whose initials these are. Ff. 1 and 2 contain some notes that according to a heading were written by Bishop Peder Hersleb (1689–1757), about the Edda in general and about this manuscript in particular:

> Om dette Exemplars store Raritet er dette at sige, at neppe i heele Island skal findes 2 a 3 gode Exemplarer af denne Edda, men denne er confereret med et Exemplar den lærde Sa. Eyulfur Jonssen eiede, og et andet Lavmand Widalin har hafft og altsaa er meget accurat . . .

1866 thus belongs to the group of manuscripts derived from one that had been collated with Eyjólfur Jónsson's manuscript, i.e. from Jón Egilsson's manuscript. We are informed that it had been copied from the 'membr.' (i.e. the Codex Regius), but there are also included variants from Hauksbók and AM 748 I a 4to. First there are the poems from the Codex Regius in their original order. After *Hamðismál* is written 'Finis' with a tracery ornament after it. Then follow *Hrafnagaldur* (pp. 321–324, ff. 161r–162v), *Baldrs draumar*, *Fjölsvinnsmál*, *Hyndluljóð*, *Gróugaldur*, *Grottasǫngr*, *Heiðreks gátur*, *Sólarljóð* and *Sonatorrek*. This part of the manuscript is written in a different hand from that of the preceding poems. *Hrafnagaldur* is arranged in unnumbered eight-line stanzas.

1866 has the poems in a different order from that of the other manuscripts that are derived from Jón Egilsson's manuscript. In *Hrafnagaldur* it reproduces the error in stanza division in stt. 20–21, and also the corrections 'Ragna' (st. 19) and 'Man*n*heim' (st. 24), marked 'forte', and it has the same variant readings from paper manuscripts as 1492, 773 a and 1109 ('al'), but no variants marked 'c.E.' (Eyjólfur Jónsson's manuscript).

1866 reproduces the same distinctive readings of B as 1109, 1492 and 773 a, and has the following innovations in common with them: st. 15, 'mar' and st. 21, 'syan*n*a'. But the innovation in st. 9, 'virir' (found in all three), is not found in 1866, which here reads 'vidrir' (this could of course be an independent correction made by a scribe who was familiar with the names of Norse mythology). The error in st. 26, 'mola', which is found in 1492 and 773 a, does not appear in 1866 either (though this only involves a misreading of minims). So it seems likely that this manuscript is not derived from any of these three. 1866 has a few distinctive readings of its own: st. 14, 'svrmi' and 'orun*n*' (instead of 'svimi' and 'ǫrvit'), st. 15, 'Jiorna' and 'jiotnum', st. 20, 'ragu' (instead of 'fragu'), that are not found elsewhere in this sub-group. It was perhaps derived from Jón Egilsson's manuscript independently of 1109, 773a and 1492 via a sister manuscript of the source of those three.

1866 has been in the collections of Luxdorph and Suhm (Suhm no. 28 4to). It was used and called Codex Luxdorphianus in *Edda* 1787–1828, II xxviii, and *Norrœn fornkvæði* 1867, xlvi; xlix; lii; lvi–vii), where it has the siglum L (lvi).[25] The manuscript is mentioned in Jónas Kristjánsson 1987.

Ms Icel. 47, Harvard University Library (47)
This manuscript has 189 leaves, plus two extra ones at the beginning and one at the end, bound in calf with gold tooling and a stamp in gold and

[25] See Bugge's note on the use of this manuscript in the Arnamagnæan edition: 'Betegnelsen af dette og andre Hskrr. i Edda Sæm. ed. AM. er meget forvildende: i Tom. II anføres Læsemaader af Codex Luxdorphianus (No. 1866) under mærket „L.", medens „L." i Tom. I betegner Codex Langebekianus; og Tom II, p. xxviii findes om Cod. Suhmianus anført det som gjælder Cod. Luxd.' (1867, lvi, note 1).

red. Ff. 34r–v, 39v–40v, 46r–v, 51v, 59v, 69v, 95r–v, 105v, 114r–v, 117v, 121r–v, 186v are all blank. The manuscript is described in Shaun Hughes's unpublished catalogue (1977) of Icelandic manuscripts in the Houghton Library, Harvard University.

This manuscript is the so-called Codex Ericianus. It was written by Jón Eiríksson between 1765 and 1775 and bears the title 'Edda Sæmundi Froda vulgo sic dicta' on f. 2r, followed by a note on the transcription. Jón Eiríksson with this manuscript prepared the foundation for Guðmundur Magnússon's edition of *Hrafnagaldur* in *Edda* 1787–1828, I.

According to information at the beginning of the manuscript, George Stephens (1813–1895), the British scholar and collector, bought it from Bernhard Rosenblad's collection in January 1845. On the inside of the cover Rosenblad wrote his name and the date 22/8 1831. On the recto of the front flyleaf is written: 'Sæmund's Edda. A valuable Text drawn up by some Danish Northern Scholar about 1770. Of great importance for any future Edition of the Edda. Bought from the Collection of the Chamberlain Bernhard Rosenblad, Stockholm, January 5, 1845'. On f. 1r is written in Swedish and with a pencil, probably in Rosenblad's hand: 'Skrifven af Jon Erikson Over-Bibliothekarie Kjøbenhavn. 1760–70-talet'. On the same page is written in Danish by a different hand: 'Dette Haandskrift omtales i Arnamagnæanske Udgave af Sæmundar Edda I Side xliii & Bugges Udg S. lxi'. The manuscript was procured for the Houghton Library by The Longfellow Fund in November 1937. It had originally been in Jón Eiríksson's possession, and in the auction catalogue of his books after his death, Bibliotheca Ericiana, appears according to Hughes under no. 632.

On f. 1r Jón Eiríksson wrote a note, explaining which manuscripts he had collated and based his edition on. The variants marked 'P.S.' come from a paper manuscript written by Páll Sveinsson. This manuscript had the same readings as D, and is probably identical with it. D was owned by Thott, and Jón may have gained access to it in Copenhagen. Jón Eiríksson states that he has in addition given variants, marked 'Sv', 'C.S.' and 'S', from a copy with the inscription 'Finitum Holmiæ in posterioribus Idibus Maj a$^{\underline{o}}$ 1684'. This must be identical with 1870, which is a copy of 34, Helgi Ólafsson's copy of A. Jón Eiríksson would have had access to this manuscript in Copenhagen.

In *Edda* 1787–1828, II xvii–xx there is a register of the order of the poems in Codex Svecus (1870), Codex Langebekianus and Codex Luxdorphianus (1866) taken from Codex Ericianus (47), f. 1v–2v (cf. Hughes 1977, 91). 47 has the poems in the following order: *Baldrs draumar*, *Grottasǫngr*, *Gróugaldr*, *Fjölsvinnsmál*, *Hyndluljóð*, *Vǫlundarkviða*, *Alvíssmál*. Then follow the heroic poems in the Codex Regius order, and after *Hamðismál* come *Hrafnagaldur* and *Sólarljóð*. In 1866 *Hrafnagaldur* comes after *Hamðismál* and before *Baldrs draumar*, and in Codex Langebekianus it is missing.

Hrafnagaldur in 47 is probably a copy of 1866, even though the two manuscripts do not have the poems in the same order. Of the extant manuscripts containing *Hrafnagaldur*, only these two have the following innovations compared with B: st. 14, 'orunn' instead of 'ǫrvit', st. 15, 'Jiorna' and 'jiotnum', st. 20, 'ragu' (for 'fragu'), though 47 has corrected the error in stanza division in stt. 20–21.

47 was used to establish the text in the Arnamagnæan edition (see *Edda* 1787–1828, I xlii–xliii). Bugge mentions 47 in *Norrœn fornkvæði*, 1867, lxi), but he did not have direct access to it. At that time it was in the possession of George Stephens (Hughes 1977, 91). But Bugge states that he has included a few readings from 'Erichsens håndskrift' taken from the Arnamagnæan edition.

Adv. 21.4.7, National Library of Scotland (21.4.7)

This manuscript has 285 leaves, is half-bound in leather and contains eddic poems. On f. 1r it bears the title 'Edda Sæmundar Prests ins Froþa Sigfussonar at Odda'. Apart from the poems *Rígsþula* and *Hǫfuðlausn,* the manuscript is in a single hand which has also added variant readings in the margin in various places. From *Rígsþula* onwards the text is written in two columns. Ff. 5–284 were numbered early on as nos. 1–280, and f. 3v is blank. On the last page the initials 'M: E S' are written twice.

The manuscript came into the collection in Edinburgh from Finnur Magnússon, who wrote on the front flyleaf: 'Edda Sæmundina | sive poëtica | (proprie sic dicta. | additis pluribus borealis vetust-|tis carminibus)'.[26] There is no information in the manuscript about when or by whom it was written, but according to Ólafur Halldórsson, who has drawn up an unpublished catalogue (1967) of Icelandic manuscripts in Edinburgh, it was written c. 1750 by a scribe who was probably from Sauðlauksdalur, and it may have been Eggert Ólafsson (1726–1768).

On ff. 2r–3r there is a list of contents, but it does not correspond to the order of the poems in the manuscript. In the actual manuscript, there are first the poems of the Codex Regius in their original order, and after *Hamðismál*

---

[26] In an article on Finnur Magnússon's sale of Icelandic manuscripts to the British Library, Pamela Porter cites a document that Finnur Magnússon sent in 1830 to the author and diplomat John Bowring (1792–1872), now preserved in the British Library (Add. 29537), where he speaks of a sale of 56 manuscripts to the Advocates Library in 1826 for £120 (Porter 2006, 181). But it is not certain that 21.4.7 was one of these.

come *Rígsþula*, *Hrafnagaldur*, *Baldrs draumar*, *Fjölsvinnsmál*, *Hyndluljóð*, *Gróugaldur*, *Grottasǫngr*, *Heiðreks gátur*, *Sólarljóð*, *Sonatorrek* and *Hǫfuðlausn*. The order of the poems not in the Codex Regius is the same as in 1866, except for *Rígsþula* and *Hǫfuðlausn*, which are not in 1866, but these poems, as stated above, are in a different hand. The order of the poems also corresponds to that in 4877, though that manuscript does not have the two poems of Egill Skallagrímsson.

Hrafnagaldur is on ff. 253r–257r. It is, apart from stt. 20 and 21, where the mistake in stanza division is reproduced, arranged in unnumbered eight-line stanzas. Shared readings show that 21.4.7 must be closely related to the sub-group of manuscripts derived from the one collated with Eyjólfur Jónsson's manuscript (1109, 1492, 773 a and 1866). It shares 'mar' in st. 15 with 1109, 1492, 773 a and 1866, and gives the correction 'Ragna' for 'rakna' in the margin by st. 19. Like 1866, it does not share 'virir' in st. 9 and 'mola' in st. 26 with 1492 and 773 a, having 'viþrir' and 'nióla' instead, and it has 'svrmi' in st. 14 like 1866 and 47. But the readings of 1866 and 47 in st. 15, 'Jiorna' and 'jiotnum', are not found in 21.4.7. It has a few readings superior to 1866 and 47, e.g. 'ǫrvit' in st. 14 (against their 'orunn') and 'fragu' in st. 20 (where 1866 and 47 have 'ragu'). In st. 11 it has the innovation 'burdar' (for 'burda'). The differences between 21.4.7 and 1866 indicate that neither can be copied from the other, but the readings they have in common show that there is a close relationship. The letter forms and arrangement of *Hrafnagaldur* in 21.4.7 are also very similar to those in 1866. It is likely that 21.4.7 is a sister manuscript to 1866, and perhaps they both derive from Jón Egilsson's manuscript via a lost intermediary.

Add. MS. 4877, British Library (4877)

This manuscript has 228 leaves and was written in the eighteenth century. It contains a Sæmundar Edda, 'Edda Sæmundar prestz ins froda Sigfussonar', and has variant readings from other paper manuscripts in the margins. It is in the Banks Collection in the British Library. When Sir Joseph Banks returned home from his journey to Iceland in 1772, he had with him a number of manuscripts and printed books that he had acquired, among them 4877, and he presented them to the British Museum in December the same year (*The British Library: Catalogue of Additions to the Manuscripts 1756–1782*, 234–235).

After the poems that are in the Codex Regius, there follow *Hrafnagaldur* (188v–192v), *Baldrs draumar*, *Fjölsvinnsmál*, *Hyndluljóð*, *Gróugaldur*, *Grottasǫngr*, *Heiðreks gátur* and *Sólarljóð*. This order is the same as in 1866, but 4877 does not have *Sonatorrek* after *Sólarljóð* like 1866 and 21.4.7, nor does it have *Rígsþula* or *Hǫfuðlausn* which are both in 21.4.7.

4877 has the same divergences from B as 1109, 1492, 733 a, 1866, 47 and 21.4.7. Like those it does not have the two distinctive readings of B, 'normr' in st. 1 (where it reads 'norner') and 'hardbaþins miðir' (for 'hardbadms under') in st. 7. It shows greater affinity with 1866 and 21.4.7 than with 1109, 1492 and 773 a. In contrast to these three it has (like 1866, 47 and 21.4.7) 'vidrer' in st. 9 (not 'virir'). It also shares the reading 'svrme' in st. 14 with 1866, 47 and 21.4.7. It is closer to 21.4.7 than to 1866 and 47: 1866 and 47 have 'Jiorna' and 'jiotnum' in st. 15, where 21.4.7 and 4877 have 'Jorna' and 'jotnum'. In st. 20, 1866 and 47 have 'ragu', where 21.4.7 and 4877 have 'fragu'. In st. 14, 1866 and 47 have 'orun*n*', but here 4877, like 21.4.7, has 'ǫrvit'. 4877 and 21.4.7 share the innovation 'burdar' in st. 11. 4877 seems to be a copy of 21.4.7. That the reverse is less likely is shown by the fact that 4877 does not have the error in stanza division in stt. 20 and 21 that 21.4.7 has.

ZCJ22, English Faculty Library, Oxford (22)
This manuscript, which was written in the eighteenth century, consists of 328 leaves. It contains mainly eddic poems. It has most recently been described by Einar G. Pétursson, who has put his findings at the disposal of the present investigator. According to a typewritten slip in the front, the manuscript comes 'From the library of Robert Steele Wandsworth Common'. At the side of this slip stands the name 'Sigurður Vigfússon', who was Guðbrandur Vigfússon's brother. Guðbrandur Vigfússon held a post at Oxford University, and must have brought the manuscript to Britain with him. It is now held at the English Faculty Library on permanent loan from Christ Church.

At the beginning of the manuscript a list is given of the contents as far as *Fáfnismál*. In the same hand as this list, under the name of Sigurður Vigfússon, is written in pencil: 'See Corpus Poeticum Boreale cap. 12', i.e. Guðbrandur Vigfússon and Frederick York Powell 1883, though 'cap. 12' appears to be a mistake. On the next leaf in a different hand there is a list of contents covering the whole manuscript under the heading 'Contents | The "Sæmundar" Edda + other poems'. A third hand has written the poems themselves in Gothic script.

The first poem in the manuscript is *Vǫluspá*, and on the first page of its text is written 'possidet', and later in the same line 'Magnussen'. According to Einar G. Pétursson this presumably means either Skúli or Kristján Magnussen, who were successors of Magnús Ketilsson (1732–1803), sheriff in Búðardalur on Skarðsströnd. Underneath is written: 'Kom mier ad gióf mags míns ⟨. . .⟩ C. Magnússonar. affirmat JEggertsson'. Here the reference is to Jón Eggertsson (1800–1880), domestically educated farmer in Ytri-Fagridalur on Skarðsströnd. He was married to Kristín Skúladóttir, who was sister of Kristján Magnussen Skúlason (1801–1871; see Jón Guðnason 1961, II 350). The manuscript must have been on Skarðsströnd in the nineteenth century. According to Einar G. Pétursson, it is probable that Guðbrandur Vigfússon got it from there, and that it may have been written in connection with Magnús Ketilsson's interest in the Edda.[27]

The manuscript contains the usual eddic poems in the order of the Codex Regius. After *Hamðismál* follow *Hrafnagaldur*, *Baldrs draumar*, *Fjölsvinnsmál*, *Hyndluljóð*, *Grottasǫngr*, *Heiðreks gátur*, *Sólarljóð*, after which there are some blank pages, then Snorri Sturluson's *Háttatal*, *Háttalykill* Þorláks Guðbrandssonar Vídalíns, *Aldarháttur* and *Jómsvíkingadrápa*.

Hrafnagaldur is written on ff. 218v–223v and arranged in unnumbered eight-line stanzas. It does not have the error in stanza division in stt. 20 and 21. The manuscript has the eddic poems down to and including *Sólarljóð* in the same order as 1866 and 4877, but does not have either of Egill Skallagrímsson's poems. The text of *Hrafnagaldur* is virtually identical with that of 4877, apart from minimal orthographical differences (in st. 11, 22 has 'aldurtila' where 4877 has 'aldrtila', in st. 13, 22 has 'med', but 4877 'með', in st. 20, 22 has 'maltid', but 4877 'máltíd', and in st 26, 22 has 'nióla', but 4877 'niola'). In addition there are minor palæographical differences: 22 uses *r* rotunda more frequently than 4877. 22 might be a copy of 4877, or maybe vice versa. It seems more likely that one is a copy of the other than that they were both copied from 21.4.7, since the two have greater similarity with each other than either does with 21.4.7. Whereas 21.4.7 generally uses 'i' in inflectional endings, the other two use 'e', e.g. in st. 19, 21.4.7 has 'raþi', but the two others have 'rade', and st. 23, 21.4.7 has 'gilldi', but the two others have 'gillde'. Whereas 21.4.7 generally uses 'þ' medially and finally, 22 and 4877 have a greater tendency to use 'd' or 'ð'. Further, 21.4.7 has the error in stanza division in stt. 20 and 21 which neither 22 nor 4877 has.

NKS 1108 fol. (1108)

This manuscript, which consists of 201 leaves, bears the title 'Edda | Sęmundar Prestz | Ens | Froþa' with the letters in black, green, red and yellow. Titles of poems are written in red. F. 138 is blank. On the flyleaf is written: 'Af Bibliotheca Hytardalensi 1769 exscripta af Arna Bodvari Poët.

---

[27] Magnús Ketilsson studied at Copenhagen University and was one of the educated Icelanders of his time. Among other things he compiled several genealogies. See Þorsteinn Þorsteinsson 1935 and Eyvind Finsen 1944. Manuscripts that bear witness to his interest in the Edda are AM 916 4to and NKS 1878 a 4to.

Island.' In other words, the manuscript was written in Hítardalur in 1769 by the *ríma* poet Árni Böðvarsson (1713–1776), who lived at Akrar on Mýrar.

1108 contains the poems of the Codex Regius in the same order as in that manuscript, and after that *Baldrs draumar*, *Fjölsvinnsmál*, *Hyndluljóð*, *Gróugaldur*, *Sólarljóð* and *Hrafnagaldur* on pp. 269–274 (ff. 134r–137v). Then there is a blank leaf, followed by *Grottasǫngr* and *Heiðreks gátur*. *Hrafnagaldur* is arranged in unnumbered eight-line stanzas. According to Einar G. Pétursson, 1108 is a copy of Lbs 214 4to, which was written in Hítardalur in the first half of the eighteenth century by Jón Halldórsson and his son Vigfús (1706–1776). That manuscript, however, contains neither *Hrafnagaldur* nor *Grottasǫngr* (Einar G. Pétursson 2007, 149), so these two poems must have been copied from a different source.

Hrafnagaldur in 1108 shares some innovations with the group of manuscripts derived from one collated with Eyjólfur Jónsson's manuscript and so must be related to them. It does not, however, give any variant readings or corrections to the text of *Hrafnagaldur*, which they do. Like that group, it reproduces the following distinctive readings of B: st. 3, 'Þrains', st. 9, 'sumni', st. 13, 'a/ndgarþ', st. 19, 'Mimis', st. 23, 'mosar', st. 26, 'ulfrimar'. But like them it does not share all B's readings, and has 'nornir' in st. 1, where B has 'normr', and in st. 7, 'harþbaþms undir', where B has 'hardbaþins miðir'. Unlike 1109, 1492 and 773 a, it does not have the innovation 'virir' in st. 9, and in st. 15 it has both 'jotnom' and 'mar' and in st. 21 'syanna'. So it seems to be more closely related to 1866 and 21.4.7 than to 1109, 1492, and 773 a. In st. 14, 1108 has 'svrmi' like 1866, but not 'orun*n*' like that manuscript in the same stanza. In that place 21.4.7 has 'ǫrvit', but also has 'svrmi'. 'Svrmi' is the only one of the distinctive readings of 1866 and 21.4.7 that is found in 1108, so it cannot be a copy of either of them. I have suggested above that 21.4.7 is a sister manuscript to 1866. Besides, both these give variant readings or corrections in the margins, which 1108 does not. This also implies that 1108 is not derived from either of them. But it does have some distinctive readings of its own, in st. 3, 'þar' (for 'þur') and 'gruma' (for 'guma'), st. 8, 'ei' (for 'í'), st. 11, 'En fra vitri' (for 'Frá en vitri'), st. 15, 'munde' (for 'mun þó'). In st. 12, it has 'mẹli', where the other manuscripts have the abbreviation ('mẹl*t*i'). It looks as though 1108 is a sister manuscript or a copy of a sister manuscript to the common original of 1866 and 21.4.7 that was derived from a lost copy of Jón Egilsson's manuscript.

1108 was once in the possession of Frederik Christian Sevel (1723–1778), whence it was sold by auction in 1781 (Jón Helgason 1970, 118). Later it was in Suhm's collection (no. 394 fol.) and was used by Bugge in *Norrœn fornkvæði* 1867 (see pp. xlvi; xlix; lx–xi), where it was assigned the siglum B.

Add. 11165, *British Library* (11165)
This manuscript, which has 157 leaves in quarto format, was written in the eighteenth century. On f. 2r it has the title: 'Edda Sęmundar Prestz ens fróþa Sigfúss Sonar'. On the flyleaf is written 'Purch.ᵈ of Prof. Finn Magnussen July 1837'. It was one of the many manuscripts purchased by Frederic Madden, who was deceived about their value, for the British Library from Finnur Magnússon in 1837 for the collective price of £180 (cf. Porter 2006, 177).

It contains a collection of eddic poems. On f. 1v there is a table of contents for this manuscript. First are the Codex Regius poems, then *Baldrs draumar*, *Fjölsvinnsmál*, *Hyndluljóð*, *Grougaldur*, *Sólarljóð*, *Grottasǫngr*, *Heiðreks gátur* and finally *Hrafnagaldur*. The manuscript is written in two hands, the first wrote all the poems except *Hrafnagaldur*; this was written by the second hand.

Variants are given to *Hávamál* from 'Membr'. These are the only variants given in brackets in the margin. Some variants are given for poems not in the Codex Regius, beginning with *Baldrs draumar*, marked 'al.', but there are none for *Hrafnagaldur*.

Hrafnagaldur is arranged in unnumbered eight-line stanzas on ff. 155r–157r. Its text is virtually identical to that in 21.4.7, except that it does not have the innovation 'burdar' in st. 11 and has 'ei' in st. 8, like 1108, so neither of these two manuscripts can be derived from the other. It is shown above that 21.4.7, 1866 and 1108 are closely related. Compared with 1109, 1492 and 773 a, 1866 has the distinctive readings 'svrmi' and 'orun*n*' in st. 14, 'Jiorna' and 'jiotnum' in st. 15 and 'ragu' in st. 20. 11165 has 'svrmi' and 'jǫtnum', but not the others. 1108 also has 'jotnum' and 'svrmi', but like 21.4.7 has 'ǫrvit' and not 'orunn'. 1108 has some distinctive readings: st. 3, 'þar', 'gruma', st. 8, 'ei', st. 11, 'En fra vitri' and st. 15, 'munde'. Of these, 11165 reproduces 'ei', but not the others. It thus shares some readings with 1866, 21.4.7 and 1108, but also has one reading in common with 1108 not shared by 1866 and 21.4.7, so it is likely that it is a sister manuscript of 1108, derived from a sister manuscript of the common original of 1866 and 21.4.7 (or is perhaps a sister manuscript of the common original of 1866 and 21.4.7, and 1108 is derived from it).

Another sub-group within the B group consists of the manuscripts 648, 1588 a I and II, 1689, 643, 21.5.2, 329 and 1111. These manuscripts share a number of innovations compared with B, for example 'gornar' (st. 3), 'linnit' (st. 5), 'biuþa' (st. 11) and 'yggioagi' (st. 18), and all have the same error in line division in st. 18 ('vallda báþo sęta | at sumbli sitia').

JS 648 4to (648)
This manuscript consists of three pages containing a table of contents + 122 pages, bound in paper and cloth. The existing manuscript comprises parts of several originally different manuscripts and seems to be written by seven different hands. On f. 1r stands the title 'Ljóda-Safn' and underneath 'XVI. bindi'. A number of leaves that were damaged at the edges have been repaired. In *Hrafnagaldur* the edges of the leaves have crumbled away, but the text that had gone has been inserted by a later hand on different paper that has been pasted in.

The existing manuscript contains various poems. The first part contains a list of Danish kings, the second part *rímur* composed by Árni Böðvarsson (who also wrote 1108), Árni Þorkelsson (*Rímur af hvarfi og drukknan árið 1768 Eggerts skálds Ólafssonar*), Gísli Konráðsson, Hallgrímur Pétursson, Hildibrandur Arason, Jón Jónsson skon, Jón Sigurðsson Dalaskáld Gíslasonar (or his father), Sigurður Breiðfjörð, Sigurður skáldi Jónsson and Þórarinn Jónsson. The third part contains *Krosskvæði* and *Maríuvísur*. The last part contains eddic poems: *Hárbarðsljóð*, *Sólarljóð*, *Hrafnagaldur* (in the manuscript's present state on ff. 60v–61r) and finally the beginning of *Vafþrúðnismál*. This part was probably written in the early eighteenth century.

Hrafnagaldur is arranged in unnumbered stanzas with the lines separated by commas but written continuously like prose, though it still has the error in stanza division in stt. 20 and 21. Its text is closely related to that in B, and may be derived from B via a lost intermediate manuscript. It does not reproduce the distinctive readings of B in st. 1, 'normr', where it has 'nornir', and st. 7, 'hardbaþins', where it has 'harbaþins', but it does reproduce all the others.

648 has the following innovations: st. 3, 'gornar' (for 'grunar'), st. 5, 'linnit' (for 'linnir'), st. 11, 'biuþa' (for 'burþa'), st. 14, 'giðrvallt i' (for 'giorvallri'), st. 18, 'yggioagi' (for 'yggiongi') and st. 22, 'ockar' (for 'orkar'). It seems to be related to 1588 a I and II and 1689, and Verri, who examined these manuscripts in 2007 (40–41), believed that 1588 a I and II and 1689 went back to a sister manuscript to 648.

Lbs 1588 a 4to (1588 a)
This manuscript has 151 leaves plus three slips inserted at the beginning, and contains among other things two collections of eddic poems. Ff. 41, 42 and 43 are blank. According to the catalogue, it was written c. 1770, mostly by vice-principal Halldór Hjálmarsson (1745–1805). A passage about the

sheriffs in Dalasýsla at the end of the existing manuscript was written by Bogi Benediktsson of Staðarfell (1771–1849), who now owned the manuscript. Some letters to Halldór Hjálmarsson from Engilbert Jónsson (1747–1820) and Halldór's brothers Erlendur (1750–1835) and Páll (1752–1830) accompanied it at that time, and these are now preserved separately as Lbs 1588 b 4to. Among these is one to Þorgrímur T⟨hor⟩láksson from Páll Andrésson. The earliest of the letters is from 1769, the latest 1774. 1588 a is in a poor state and has been put together from four different original manuscripts. It is now wrapped in a piece of leather that was once used for binding.

Inserted in the front of the manuscript is a list of contents and a table of 'hve Fingal var gamall þegar hinir og þessir atburðir gerðust'. They are written by different hands. In the list of contents *Hrafnagaldur* is the second poem in the collection, standing between *Sólarljóð* and *Hávamál*. After *Loddfáfnismál* in this list is added in parantheses: 'qvod noto (inqvid Vidalinus) si forte Sveci ita vocent aut citent caput aliqvod Sæmundar eddu, vix aliud Mysterium suberit'. This note, which is here attributed to Páll Vídalín, must refer to Helgi Ólafsson's annotations in B, which was probably in Páll Vídalín's possession. But the list of contents cannot apply to 1588 a 4to, for the poems in the manuscript are not written in the same order as they are listed here. On the verso of the leaf containing the list of contents it reads: 'Kvidur | Sæmundar | Eddu | B.H.S.' This may refer to Bjarni Halldórsson (1703–1773), sheriff at Þingeyrar,[28] who in all likelihood owned a Sæmundar Edda that had belonged to Vídalín. 1109 is derived from a manuscript that had been collated with a paper manuscript in Bjarni Halldórsson's possession, but no readings are given for *Hrafnagaldur* that correspond to 1109, so it may be another manuscript that is referred to.

The first section of the existing 1588 a contains two prefaces to Snorri's *Edda* ('Edda Íslendinga'), of which one is a new prologue to Snorris *Edda* with a discussion of the manuscripts of the Edda by Eggert Ólafsson (cf. Faulkes 1979, 143). Then follows 'Nomenclaturæ vocum Grammaticarum Eddu authoris'.

The second section, written in a different hand, contains the end of *Hǫfuðlausn*, *Hrafnagaldur* (ff. 9r–10v), 'Vijsur Einars Skúla sonar um hin*ar* nafnkunnugre Eijar vid Noreg űr Notis Olavi Verelii yfer Hervarar Sogu' (an extract from the *Laufás Edda*; written in the same hand as *Hrafnagaldur*).

The third section, written in a third hand, has on f. 13r Vigfús Scheving's name. This is probably Vigfús Scheving Hansson (1735–1817), who left

---

[28] This is Verri's suggestion.

Introduction 53

Hólaskóli in 1754 and studied in Copenhagen.[29] On f. 13v is an account of the source of the fourth section:

> Þesse Sæm. Edda er skrifud epter Eddu Próf. S*ira* Po. H.S. er h*ann* m*ed* eigen*n* hende hef*ur* skrifad eptir Exempl. Vice L.m. sal. E.O.S. (er meinaz m*ed* h*onum* forgenged hafe) hún er af mi*er* sam*an* boren*n* vid eitt an*n*ad Exemplar, gott ad sön*n*u, en*n* hyrdula/sl. skrifad, hvar f*yrer* þ*ar* s*em* þetta mismunadi fra því, og mier virdtiz þad þo vera rettara, en*n* þesse, sette eg variantem, og an*n*adhvert f. hiá, ed*ur* forte. Sid*an* bar eg hana sam*an* vid eitt gott Exemplar i 4to, er eg meina hafe verid lögm. P. Widalins, og sie af h*onom* completerad, hefur þad ádur att Sira Helge, er hingad og þangad hef*ur* inn í þ*ad* teiknad eitt og an*n*ad, og mun h*ann* hafa fært þad hingad úr Svíaríke; Exemplarid er bædi gott og gamallt, en*n* upp á orthographiam er þad grej-korn. Þar fyrer, þar s*em* her stend*ur* þetta Teikn 4) merker þ*ad*, ad so standi á tiedu Exempl.

The manuscript that had belonged to Páll Vídalín and Helgi Ólafsson must, as pointed out above, be B, where it is stated in the list of contents that Helgi Ólafsson had made annotations in the manuscript. It is assumed that Helgi must have brought the manuscript with him from Sweden to Iceland. On f. 14v there is another list of contents of a Sæmundar Edda, in which *Hrafnagaldur* comes between *Hyndluljóð* and *Vǫlundar- kviða*. On f. 15r there is again a note on the source and the copying method that had been used. The explanations in the two places (f. 13v and f. 15r) are written in the same hand, perhaps that of Halldór Hjálmarsson.

> Þar s*em* an*n*adhvert á sjalfre þessare Eddubók, ed*ur* fylgiande bæklíng*ur* fyrer kemur þetta teikn 4) þá merker þ*ad* eitt agætt exe*m*pl. í 4to, er siáanlega var skrifad epter sömu bók og Jóns Ól. Edda, en líklega miklu fyrre, þad hefi eg med nockurn vegen*n* gætni samanlesed vid þetta mitt, og merkt þetta 4) þvi ad so stande í þeir*ri* bók, sem þad tilvisar ... Þykiz eg hafa vered nærga/ngull í þessu, og skrifad líka, þad sem 4) hefur út á spatiun*n*e, þeg*ar* eitt ord kan*n* ad hafa radiz á tvo vegu.

On f. 16r there is another list of contents for a Sæmundar Edda, written in another hand, but here *Hrafnagaldur* is not mentioned. Then follows a preface to Snorri's *Edda*, other writings about the Edda in Icelandic and Latin, a genealogy from Óðinn to the kings of Norway and an epilogue to the Edda. These mythological items are in the hand of Einar Hálfdanarson (1695–1753), as is stated on f. 40v.

The fourth section of the existing manuscript contains a Sæmundar Edda, written in a new hand. Here there are loose leaves with notes inserted

---

[29] This might alternatively be the farmer Vigfús Scheving Jónsson (1749–1834), who was also educated at Hólaskóli.

among the poems. The poems as far as and including *Þrymskviða* are in the order of Codex Regius. Then follow *Baldrs draumar*, *Grottasǫngr*, *Gróugaldur*, *Fjölsvinnsmál*, *Hyndluljóð* and *Hrafnagaldur* (ff. 77r–78v),[30] after which from *Vǫlundarkviða* to *Hamðismál* inclusive are written in the order of the Codex Regius. Then come *Rígsþula* and *Sólarljóð* (followed by a Latin translation). Last in this section is the above-mentioned passage about the sheriffs in Dalasýsla.

The list of contents on f. 14v has the poems in an order that corresponds with the order in which the poems are written in this fourth section of the manuscript. *Hrafnagaldur* here also has variants marked '4)' or '|: . . . :|' or '(: . . . :)'. Those with the last are identical with the variants that we find in 1689. The accounts of the source on ff. 13v and 15r and the list of contents on f. 14v must all apply to this part of the manuscript.

It will have been noticed that the manuscript has *Hrafnagaldur* in two different places (in the second and fourth sections) and in two different hands. I label these two versions 1588 a I and 1588 a II.

1588 a I has *Hrafnagaldur* arranged in unnumbered stanzas mostly of 8 lines with some confusion in line breaks, suggesting that its original had the poem written out as prose. It also has the mistake in stanza division in stt. 20 and 21. It reflects the innovations in 648. Like 648, 1588 a I does not reproduce B's reading 'normr' for 'nornir' in st. 1, and in st. 7 it has 'harbaðins', like 648, instead of B's 'hardbaþins'. It shares the following innovations with 648: st. 3, 'gornar' (for 'grunar'), st. 5, 'lin*n*it' (for 'linnir'), st. 7, 'miðir' (for 'undir'), st. 11, 'biuþa' (for 'burþa'), st. 14, 'giørvallt i' (for 'giorvallri'), and st. 18, 'yggioagi' (for 'Yggiongi').

1588 a I has the following innovations compared with 648, which shows that 648 cannot be derived from it, for example: st. 8, 'vargsbelgs ellðu' (for 'vargsbelg seldu', though this is written as one word in 648), st. 14, 'svimt' (for 'svimi'), st. 15, 'kotaran*n*' (for 'komin*n*'), and st. 23, 'hrat' (for 'hropt'). So 1588 a I could be a copy of 648, or be derived from a sister manuscript.

The text of 1588 a I has some readings that are given as variants (written within brackets and enclosed in colons thus '(: . . . :)') in 21.5.2, 1111, 1689 and 1588 a II (cf. st. 5, 'linnit'). Some variants given in these manuscripts are also found in other manuscripts besides 1588 a I (thus st. 1, 'þiæ', which is also found in 21.6.7 and 966 and the A group and in B, and st. 17, 'ǫlteiti'). 1588 a I cannot have been the text from which these variants were taken, since it has the obviously corrupt forms 'baðins' in

---

[30] In this part of the existing 1588 a the leaves are numbered at the top right of each leaf. According to this numbering *Hrafnagaldur* is on ff. 34r–35v.

st. 7 and 'yggioagi' in st. 18, while those manuscripts have the correct forms ('baþms' and 'Yggiongi') as variant readings. It may be that the variants written within brackets and enclosed in colons were from various unspecified manuscripts or were suggested emendations.

1588 a I may therefore be a copy of a sister manuscript of 648 (so Verri 2007, 40), and 21.5.2, 1111, 1689 and 1588 a II may be derived from a manuscript closely related to 1588 a I.

1588 a II has *Hrafnagaldur* arranged in unnumbered eight-line stanzas. It does not have the errror in stanza division in stt. 20 and 21. It reproduces the innovations of both 648 and 1588 a I, with the exception of 'lin*n*it' in st. 5, where it has 'lin*n*ir'; 'lin*n*it' is, however, given in the margin as a variant reading, as also in 1689, 21.5.2, 329, 1111, and 643.

1588 a II has a number of innovations that are perhaps due to errors in the manuscript it was copied from (cf. the scribe's comments quoted above, which suggest that he did his work conscientiously). Innovations compared with B are found in st. 5, 'eya' (for 'eva'), st. 6, 'fa asci hnigin' (for 'frá aski hniginn'), st. 7, 'cun*n*r' (for 'kun*n*i'), st. 9, 'galt' (for 'gátt'), st. 10, 'vera' (for 'vegu'), st. 12, 'katti (for 'knatti'), st. 13, 'Ein' (for 'Eins'), st. 16, 'gymnis' (for 'g*r*imnis'), st. 17, 'alteiti' (for 'a/lteiti'), st. 18, 'seta' (for 'sæla'), st. 20, 'spalmál' (for 'spakmál'), and st. 25, 'ur þrot' (for 'und rot').

Since 1588 a II does not reproduce all the innovations of 1588 a I in its text, it is probably not copied from it, even though the one that is not in its text is in the margin (it is is likely to be from elsewhere). It may be that it is a sister manuscript to 1588 a I, though the possibility cannot be excluded that it derives from 1588 a I and a scribe has corrected the error 'linnit' in st. 5.

The innovations of 1588 a II are not found in 21.5.2, 329 or 1111, though they are in 1689 and 643. *Hrafnagaldur* in 1588 a II is closely related to the text of the poem in 1689; according to Verri they could be sister manuscripts (2007, 41–42). They are likely to have been derived from a sister manuscript to 1588 a I.

Lbs 1588 4to was discussed in Faulkes (1979, 143–144).

Lbs 1689 4to (1689)
This manuscript, which consists of vi + 246 pages, has been trimmed and half-bound in leather. According to Páll Eggert Ólafsson's catalogue it was written by Sæmundur Hólm (1749–1821). The title on the spine is 'Sæmundar EDDA'. The first leaves of the original manuscript have rotted away (as far as f. 5r), and been replaced by the beginning of *Vǫluspá* written in a later hand and on different paper from the rest of the manuscript. These

leaves were written by Þorleifur Jónsson of Skinnastaður (1845–1911). On the flyleaf he has written his name and the date: 'Þorleifr Jónsson. 1878', and on the flyleaf under his name: 'Til Bókasafns Latínuskólans 1883. Afhent Landsbókasafninu til eignar árið 1914'.

On f. 1r stands the title 'Sæmundar-edda', after which follows a list of contents, which are first the poems of the Codex Regius largely in the same order, but after *Þrymskviða* come *Baldrs draumar, Grottasǫngr, Gróugaldur, Fjölsvinnsmál, Hyndluljóð, Hrafnagaldur*, and then the rest of the Codex Regius poems (*Vǫlundarkviða* to *Hamðismál*) followed by *Sonatorrek, Merlínusspá, Krákumál, Vísa Trémanns í Sámseyju* from *Ragnars saga, Gullkársljóð, Hyndluljóð* (again), *Valagaldur Kráku. Hrafnagaldur* has the same placing between *Hyndluljóð* and *Vǫlundarkviða* in 1588 a II.

Hrafnagaldur is on ff. 50r–52r, and is the sixteenth poem in the manuscript (*Hávamál* and *Loddfáfnismál* being taken as separate poems), as noted at the beginning of the poem in Sæmundur Hólm's hand. It is arranged in unnumbered eight-line stanzas. It does not have the errror in stanza division in stt. 20 and 21. In 1689 it includes all the same innovations and marginal notes as 1588 a II and 648 (cf. the descriptions of these manuscripts), but not the variants from B that are given in 1588 a II, marked 4). Perhaps this is because 1689 and 1588 a II are sister manuscripts, both copied from a sister manuscript to 1588 a I, but it could also be because 1689 was copied from 1588 a II before these variants were added in the margin.

1689 introduces only a few innovations compared with 1588 II a: st. 3, 'ec' (for 'er'), st. 14, 'glyo' (for 'glygio'). In st. 14, it has 'ofsvimt' written as one word.

The layout of both *Hrafnagaldur* and the other poems in 1689 is largely the same as that in 643, which must have been written by the same scribe (Sæmundur Hólm). *Hrafnagaldur* is, for example, numbered 'XVI' in both. There are as far as can be seen neither errors nor anything else in these two copies that can help to judge which of the two is derived from the other.

Egerton 643, British Library (643)

This manuscript is a Sæmundar Edda in quarto format, consisting of 122 leaves witten in two columns in the eighteenth century. It was sold for £50 in October 1812 by Finnur Magnússon to Archibald Constable (1774–1827), the publisher of most of Walter Scott's works (Porter 2006, 181). It was sold on from him to Adam Clarke (died 1832). In his collection of manuscripts it bore according to Ward 1893 the number LXVII. After Clarke's death it was offered for sale by auction at Sotheby's in 1838 by Baynes & Son. The auction was cancelled because of a lack of bids, but subsequently bought, together with a manuscript of Snorri's *Edda* which became Egerton 642, by Frederic Madden for the British Museum (see Porter 2006, 184–185, 187). Before the failed auction it was advertised as: 'This beautiful perfect, and remarkably correct and distinctly written MS., may be considered as a great acquisition to this country. It contains a good and well-adjusted text of all the pieces published in the printed copies, with a great many others still more curious and interesting, which have been hitherto known only by report . . .' (quoted from Porter 2006, 183). This is identical, apart from a few details, to the beginning of the description on f. 1r of the manuscript.

On the front flyleaf Finnur Magnússon has written 'Codex Thorlacianus'. It had been owned by Børge Thorlacius, and it is from him that Finnur Magnússon got it (see Jón Helgason not yet published). F. 1r–1v contains a description of the manuscript in English. On f. 2r is a list of contents written in pencil, probably by Finnur Magnússon. According to the introduction to *Edda* 1787–1828, I, Finnur Magnússon used a manuscript he referred to as 'T.' to collate with the poems about Helgi Hundingsbani, and it is stated in *Edda* 1787–1828, II xxix that 'T.' was Codex Thorlacianus. According to Ward's catalogue, however, the readings quoted from T are not always identical with those of 643. *Edda* 1787–1828 gives no variants to *Hrafnagaldur* from 643.

643 has first the Codex Regius poems in the same order as far as and including *Þrymskviða*, then *Baldrs draumar*, *Grottasǫngr*, *Gróugaldur*, *Fjölsvinnsmál*, *Hyndluljóð* and *Hrafnagaldur* (ff. 50r–52r, pp. 99–103). Then follow *Vǫlundarkviða* and the other Codex Regius poems in the usual order. After *Hamðismál* comes *Rígsþula*. *Hrafnagaldur* is in 643 placed between *Hyndluljóð* and *Vǫlundarkviða*, as in 1588 a II and 1689. It has largely the same layout as 1689, see the description of the latter above, and has the same distinctive readings. As stated above, it cannot be determined which of the two is copied from the other. 643 is written in the same hand as 1689, which according to the catalogue was written by Sæmundur Hólm.

Adv. 21.5.2, *National Library of Scotland* (21.5.2)
This manuscript, which consists of 361 leaves, is bound in leather and has gilding on the spine, which bears the title 'Edda Sæmundi'. The manuscript is described in Ólafur Halldórsson's unpublished catalogue of Icelandic manuscripts in Edinburgh (1967). It is paginated by the original scribe as pp. 1–715 = ff. 1r–358r. On the front flyleaf is written 'quondam e libris Skulonis Theodori Thorlacii, | Islando – Dani.' That is, the manuscript was once in Skúli Thorlacius's library; it may have got there via Grímur Thorkelín (see Ólafur Halldórsson 1967).

According to Ólafur Halldórsson, 21.5.2 was written by a single hand in Iceland in 1755–1756 and in Copenhagen in 1758. Nowhere in the manuscript is it stated who wrote it, but it was probably Eggert Ólafsson (1726–1768), who matriculated from the school at Skálholt, studied at the university in Copenhagen and was employed by the Arnamagnæan Commission. As part of his duties he travelled in Iceland during the years 1752–1757. 21.5.2 is written in the same hand as 329, which according to a letter with it was probably written by Eggert (see the description of 329 below).

21.5.2 contains the eddic poems from the Codex Regius in the same order, but after *Þrymskviða* are inserted *Baldrs draumar*, *Grottasǫngr*, *Grougaldur*, *Fjölsvinnsmál* and *Hyndluljóð*. After *Hamðismál* follow *Hrafnagaldur* (pp. 455–462, ff. 228r–231v) and *Sólarljóð*. The manuscript also contains poems by Egill Skallagrímsson, as well as poems from *Heimskringla* and various fornaldarsögur. On ff. 227v, 334v and 340v there is information about the manuscripts from which it was copied. That on f. 334v concerns the original for *Merlínusspá*, on 340v the original for *Ynglingatal*, *Hornklofavísur* and *Hákonarmál*. What is written on f. 227v is of interest for *Hrafnagaldur*:

> NB. þessar efter skrifada*r* (it. ad*ur* nefnda*r* Vegtams qv. etc) kvidur, liöd og kvædi eru ür bök Sr. Vigf. J. S. Prof. i Hitardal. Á saumu bök va*r* Sæm. Edda skrifud af Sr. Jone Haldorssyne epter Eddu Arna M. S. hvöria han*n* siälfur hafde skrifad epter membrana. Þar va*r* ï bökin*n*i Sn. Edda og sïdan kvædin af hvörium ecke*rt* va*r* anneсterad Sæmu*n*dar Eddu heldur indisposité ritud, efter misjöfn*um* (sem mie*r* synist) exemplaribus.

According to this, the poems from *Hrafnagaldur* onwards (presumably including the poems by Egill and those from *Heimskringla* and fornaldarsögur), as well as *Baldrs draumar* to *Hyndluljóð*, were copied from a manuscript owned by Vigfús Jónsson of Hítardalur, which had been copied by Jón Halldórsson from Árni Magnússon's autograph copy of the Codex Regius.[31] Vigfús's manuscript also contained Snorri's *Edda*, and after that a series of poems from disparate sources (i.e. *Hrafnagaldur* and the rest).

The last part of 21.5.2 (f. 228r onwards) is according to Ólafur Halldórsson (1967, III 88) largely a copy of Lbs 214 4to, written by Jón Halldórsson and his son Vigfús Jónsson. This manuscript must be the source of the material after *Hamðismál*, but as stated above (p. 49)

---

[31] Ólafur Halldórsson (1967, 64) writes in his catalogue that the first part of 21.5.2, as far as 227v, was a copy of a manuscript belonging to Þórður Jónsson of Staðarstaður, which was copied from the Codex Regius. This cannot of course apply to the material after f. 227v.

it does not include *Hrafnagaldur*. 1108 is also a copy of a manuscript in 'Bibliotheca Hytardalensi', and according to Einar G. Pétursson, its source was also Lbs 214 4to. 1108 does not include the same poems from outside the Codex Regius as 21.5.2.

Hrafnagaldur in 21.5.2 is arranged in eight-line stanzas, and does not have the error in stanza division. The text reproduces the innovations compared with B that are found in the sub-group of manuscripts that seem to go back to a sister manuscript to 648. It includes precisely the same variants to the text as 1588 a II, 1689 and 643. It does not have the variant readings of 1588 a II from B, but these were probably added later, as suggested above, for they are written in a lighter ink though by the same hand. *Hrafnagaldur* does not, however, have the same placing in 21.5.2, as it has in 1588 a II, 643 and 1689, but the source of the text in 21.5.2 must have been closely related to those manuscripts.

21.5.2 does not reproduce the distinctive readings of 1689 and 643, whereas it does reproduce most, but not all of the distinctive readings of 1588 a II (st. 1, 'þrá', st. 5, 'eya', st. 7, 'cunnr', st. 10, 'vera', st. 16, 'gimnis', st. 17, 'alteiti', st. 18, 'sęta', and st. 25, 'ur þrot'). The readings of 1588 a II in st. 6, 'fa asci hnigin', st. 9, 'galt', st. 12, 'katti', st. 13, 'Ein' (a reading, however, written in the margin) and st. 20, 'spalmál' are not reproduced in 21.5.2, so it cannot be a copy of 1588 a II. It is possible that it is a sister to that manuscript, or derived from a sister to it.

Ms. germ. qu. 329, Staatsbibliothek zu Berlin, Preussischer Kulturbesitz (643) This manuscript, which mainly contains eddic poems, consists of 250 pages. At the front of the manuscript is inserted a letter from Rasmus Nyerup to Dr N. H. Julius, dated 22/3 1820. In this letter it says that the manuscript was probably written in Eggert Ólafsson's hand. It reads:

> ... über das isländische Manuscript, was ich hierdurch zurück zu senden die Ehre habe, vollständige Auskunft geben zu können, habe ich mir zwar Mühe gegeben, bin aber noch nicht völlig damit ins Reine gekommen. So viel ist gewiss, dass es um die Mitte ongefähr des vorigen Jahrhunderts von einem gelehrten Isländer |: wahrscheinlich dem berühmten Eggert Olafssen, der 1768 starb:| geschrieben.[32]

329 has first the poems of the Codex Regius in the same order, with the same additional poems after *Þrymskviða*. After *Hamðismál* comes *Hrafnagaldur*, followed by *Sólarljóð, Gullkársljóð, Hynduljóð, Krákumál* and finally *Jómsvíkinga drápa*. *Hrafnagaldur* is written in two columns

---

[32] Einar G. Pétursson's transcription. I have had access to photographs of the text of *Hrafnagaldur*, but not of the whole manuscript.

on pp. 207a–210a in unnumbered eight-line stanzas. The order of the poems as far as and including *Sólarljóð* is the same as in 21.5.2. Both manuscripts are written in the same hand, believed, as stated above, to be that of Eggert Ólafsson.

21.5.2 and 329 have virtually identical texts of *Hrafnagaldur*, both as regards readings, spellings and letter forms. The only differences between them are in st. 18, where 21.5.2 has the copying error 'Heila' for 'Heilan' and in st. 21, where in 329 an 'i' is written to mark the palatisation of 'g' in 'giæti'. Also the variant readings in the margins are marked 'al.' whereas in 21.5.2 they are marked '+'. It is likely that they are copies of the same original, which would have been a sister manuscript (or derived from a sister manuscript) to 1588 a II.

NKS 1111 fol. (1111)

This manuscript, which consists of 258 leaves, is from the eighteenth century. It is unbound and bears the title 'Sęmvndar-Edda' on the same page as *Vǫluspá* begins. It is written in a single hand apart from *Hrafnagaldur* and the list of contents, which are written in a second and third hand respectively.

It is clear that *Hrafnagaldur* in 1111 is copied from a different original from the other poems that are in it. They are probably partly derived from NKS 1869 4to, a Sæmundar Edda (which does not include *Hrafnagaldur*) written in the eighteenth century by Markús Jónsson, according to Kålund's catalogue. Before the table of contents (f. 257r) it says, in an account of the 'oder som Membrana ikke har': 'Den 6te Ode som kaldes Othins Ravnegalder fattedes'. The manuscript contains the eddic poems from the Codex Regius and then: *Baldrs draumar*, *Fjölsvinnsmál*, *Hyndluljóð*, *Gróugaldur*, *Sólarljóð*, *Grottasǫngr* and *Heiðreks gátur*. After that in a different hand comes *Hrafnagaldur*. This poem must have been added to the manuscript after the other poems had been written, possibly at the same time as the list of contents. The placing is perhaps therefore accidental. The poem is written in unnumbered eight-line stanzas on pp. 500–510 (ff. 250v–255v).

Variant readings are given to the text of *Hrafnagaldur*, marked 'al' or 'f' in the same way as in 329, which is not how they are in other manuscripts in this sub-group of the B group. 1111 has the same distinctive readings as 21.5.2 and 329, but it does not reproduce the error of 21.5.2 in st. 18 ('Heila'), and in st. 21 it has 'giæti', like 329. On this (admittedly flimsy) foundation rests the assumption that 1111 is a copy of 329. The two manuscripts do not, however, contain the same poems in addition to those of the Codex Regius (which is not surprising, considering that *Hrafnagaldur* in 1111 was copied from a different source from the other poems).

The manuscript was once in Suhm's collection (156 fol.). It was used by Bugge (see *Norrœn fornkvæði* 1867, lxi), where it is designated by the siglum M.

Two manuscripts of the B group both seem to be derived from an apparently lost manuscript written by Magnús Jónsson of Vigur. These are 21.6.7 and 818.

Adv. 21.6.7, National Library of Scotland (21.6.7)
This manuscript, which consists of 341 leaves, was, according to Ólafur Halldórsson's catalogue of Icelandic manuscripts in Edinburgh, written during the years 1750–1753 by Jón Egilsson (1724–1807), farmer at Stóra-Vatnshorn in Haukadalur. The existing manuscript, which was originally in three separate volumes, now bound together, has wooden covers and in many places coloured initials. On the inside of the front cover is pasted a leaf from a Sæmundar Edda in Jón Egilsson's hand, and on the inside of the back cover a letter to Jón Egilsson dated 29/10 1750 and signed 'Olafur Jonsson'.

21.6.7 begins with a preface by Jón Egilsson, in which he gives an account of his work on the manuscript and what manuscripts it was based on. The second volume, a Sæmundar Edda, which begins on f. 132r and ends on f. 257r, was, according to Jón Egilsson, a copy of a manuscript written by Magnús Jónsson (1637–1702) of Vigur on Ísafjörður. It has not been possible to identify this manuscript. It is perhaps lost. The title page of this second volume reads: 'Bookenn. | SÆMUNDAR | EDDA. | Edur. | Lioodabook Sæmundar Sigfws sonar, Pröf: ad Odda Stad. | Inne halldande forn-skaalldanna Listqvednar Lioda Dr|aapur; Dulordar og dimmkvednar forn qvidur, kiennande aa giæta Ordsnilld, Margbreittar kienningar *og* | Meistaralegar Skällda Reglur. Enn aa Nÿ uppritad, Epter Eiginn hende Magnusar | Sal: Jonssonar Er Sat I Wigur vid Isafiörd, aukenn | Nockrum ägiætum qvidumm. | Skrifud I Wogie aa Skardz strǫnd Anno 1751. | af Ione Eigils syne'.

On the title page of the third volume, f. 258r, is written: 'Jőnas Jónsson | æ Bőkena | ad Riettumm Erfdumm Epter Fødur Sinn | No. 28.' At the top is written 'Ebenezer Henderson', and on the same page: 'Her hefiast | Dulkvednar Forn | Drapur | Med Imsra | Frodra Manna | Raadning | Skrifadar Anno | 1753. | af | J: E: S:'.

The second volume of the manuscript contains *Sólarljóð*, *Hrafnagaldur* (136r–137r), *Vǫluspá*, *Hávamál*, *Vafþrúðnismál*, *Grímnismál*, *Alvíssmál*, *Lokasenna*, *Þrymskviða*, *Hárbarðsljóð*, *Skírnismál*, *Hymiskviða* and *Baldrs draumar*. Then come the heroic poems in the same order as the Codex Regius, then after *Hamðismál* follow *Fjölsvinnsmál*, *Hyndluljóð*,

Gróugaldur, Grottasǫngr, Heiðreks gátur, Egill Skallagrímsson's *Hǫfuðlausn, Hallmundar vísur, Hákonarmál, Bjarkamál,* then *Appendix,* containing *Ǫrvar-Odds drápa, Ásbjarnarkviða, Glælognskviða,* extracts from *Vellekla* and *Þórálfs drápa, Eiríksmál,* a poem by Þorbjǫrn hornklofi, stanzas by Guttormr sindri, an extract from *Gráfeldardrápa,* stanzas by Eyvindr Skáldaspillir, Gizurr gullbrárskáld, Þorfinnr munnr and Þormóðr Kolbrúnarskáld, *Noregs konungatal, Vísa trémanns í Sámseyju* from *Ragnars saga* and *Lítið ágrip um afguðina og gyðjurnar.* The poems in the first part of this second volume are in the same order as the poems in the first parts of A and B. *Hrafnagaldur* is written continuously as prose, but there is a kind of break or else a new line at the beginnings of stanzas. The stanzas are unnumbered (as in B), but the error in stt. 20 and 21 is present. The arrangement is rather reminiscent of that of A and B. The distinctive readings of B are reproduced (except for 'normr' in st. 1), so it must be derived from B. It has none of the distinctive readings of any of the sub-groups described above, so it cannot belong to any of them.

It has the following innovations: st. 2, 'þoka', st. 3, 'garnar', st. 7, 'i vistom', st. 12, 'tindwtt', st. 13, 'afatre', st. 14, 'dauþer', st. 15, 'fer'. In st. 18, 'yggunge' is written, but immediately afterwards in the text it is corrected to '/:yggionge:/'.

21.6.7 is described by Faulkes (1979, 129–131).

Lbs 818 4to (818)

This manuscript, which consists of 3 + 166 leaves, was, according to Páll Eggert Ólafsson's catalogue, written between 1750 and 1800, by four different hands. Its contents are miscellaneous. According to the catalogue, it was originally two separate manuscripts: at the bottom of the title page it says 'Samanntínt oc í eitt binde innfest og skrifad á Hrappsey 180 [sic] af Olafe Sveinssyne', and underneath 'I og II p.'. The existing volume, however, seems to consist of more than just two manuscripts, of which at least two contained eddic poems. The two parts of the existing volume are prefaced by a list of contents in Páll Pálsson's hand. Part of the volume was written by Ólafur Sveinsson (1762–1845), but the major part, according to Einar G. Pétursson (1998, 231), was written by Jón Ólafsson of Grímsstaðir in Breiðavík on Snæfellsnes (c. 1691–1765).

At the bottom of f. 46r is written 'Kolbeirn Biarnarson'. This is possibly, according to Einar G. Pétursson (1998, 232), the Kolbeinn Bjarnason who was a smallholder at Fróðá on Snæfelssnes around 1800. Landsbókasafn Íslands acquired the volume from Jón Pétursson, who according to Páll Eggert Ólason could have got it from Staðarfell, since his wife, Jóhanna Soffía Bogadóttir, came from there (Einar G. Pétursson 1998, 232).

The first part of the volume contains *Hávamál*, Kenningar og heiti, 'Siön Sira Jonz Eiölfssonar', 'Hvörnen*n* lita skal hier-lendst', 'Hvad Galld*ur* kallast', 'Um oracula', 'Upprune Galldra', 'Um Galldra Bækur', 'Afguder heidingjanna', Egill Skallagrímsson's *Hǫfuðlausn*, 'Nockrar Málsgreiner um þad hvadan Böken Edda hefir sitt nafn', 'Tillegg Nockurt heirande til Snorra Eddu, sem ecke er ad fin*n*a i þe*i*m þricktu, ütdreiged af Skrife Biörns ä Skards ä'.

The second part contains mainly eddic poems: *Heiðreks gátur, Hǫfuðlausn, Sonatorrek, Fuglagáta, Gróugaldur, Alvíssmál, Hávamál, Vǫluspá, Fjölsvinnsmál, Hymiskviða, Þrymskviða, Vafþrúðnismál, Sólarljóð, Grímnismál, Skírnismál, Lokasenna, Hyndluljóð, Hárbarðsljóð, Baldrs draumar, Sigrdrífumál, Frá dauða Sinfjǫtla, Grípisspá, Fáfnismál, Guðrúnarkviða I, Oddrúnar grátr, Vǫlundarkviða, Helgakviða Hundingsbana I, Helgakviða Hjǫrvarðssonar, Hamðismál, Sigurðarkviða in skamma, Helreið Brynhildar, Guðrúnarkviða II, Atlakviða, Atlamál in grœnlenzku*, some stanzas of *Grímnismál, Gróugaldur* (again), *Grottasǫngr* and *Guðrúnarhvǫt*. After this is a blank page (f. 77v), after which is a leaf with the final stanzas of *Atlamál in grœnlenzka* and then *Hrafnagaldur* (ff. 79v–82r) and *Guðrúnarhvǫt* (again). These four leaves seem to be written in a different hand from the other poems. The last item in the volume is *Gamla jólaskrá*, written in yet another hand.

Hrafnagaldur is arranged in eight-line stanzas. In stt. 20 and 21 there is the error in stanza division. 818 reproduces the distinctive readings of B (except for 'normr' in st. 1) and also has readings that reflect the innovations of 21.6.7: st. 3, 'garnar', st. 7, 'i vistom', st. 12, 'tind vott', st. 13, 'afatre', st. 14, 'dauþir', and st. 15, 'fer'. 818 also includes both the error ('yggungi') and its immediately following correction ('yggionge') in st. 18. There is just one that it does not reproduce, st. 2, 'þoka', which means that it is not derived from 21.6.7. In other places 818 has innovations that are not found in 21.6.7, in st. 8, 'varge belg' and 'lit om scipti', so 21.6.7 can scarcely be a copy of 818, which is also made unlikely by the arrangement of the stanzas. It is likely that the two manuscripts derive independently from the same source, which would presumably be Magnús Jónsson's manuscript. Since they do not have any of the innovations of 966, and 966 does not contain any of their innovations, Magnús Jónsson's manuscript must have been directly or indirectly derived from B.

The manuscript is described in Faulkes 1979, 115–116 and Einar G. Pétursson 1998, 231–234.

The following stemma for manuscripts in the B group seems to be possible. It is in part guesswork, since in some cases it is based on minimal differences between texts. For instance, it has not been possible to determine whether 22 is a copy of 4877 or the reverse. The same applies to 1689 and 643.

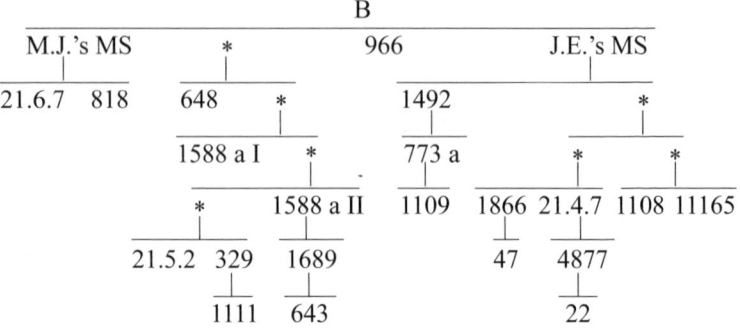

DESCRIPTION OF C

Stockholm papp. fol. nr 57 (C), which consists of 165 leaves, was written in the second half of the seventeenth century. It is half-bound in leather and the script is cursive. According to information on the front flyleaf it was bound in 1843. On the spine it bears the title 'I: Adskilianlegr Qved. 2. Saga Hakonar Hakonarsonar.' Gödel states in his catalogue that it was written by Þormóður Torfason's (Torfæus's) secretary Ásgeir Jónsson, but according to Jón Helgason (1962, xi–xiv) the scribe is unknown. It is not known how or when it got to Sweden, but it must have been already there in 1684, for in that year Helgi Ólafsson copied *Hákonar saga* from it. According to Jón Helgason (1962–1981, III xiii), it can hardly be earlier than about 1680.

The first part of the manuscript (ff. 1–10) contains eighteen narrative poems: *Cecilíu kvæði*, *Stjúpmóður minning*, *Gauta kvæði*, *Vallara kvæði*, *Bjarnasona kvæði*, *Taflkvæði*, *Bóthildar kvæði*, *Ólufar kvæði*, *Ásu dans*, *Ebba kvæði*, *Elenar ljóð*, *Marteins kviða*, *Kristínar kvæði*, *Sonar harmur*, *Þorkels kviða*, *Systra kvæði*, *Hallmundar ljóð* (with a prose introduction) and *Hrafnagaldur*. The second part (ff. 11–165) contains *Hákonar saga Hákonarsonar*.

Hrafnagaldur appears in C in a different context from that in which it is normally found. It is written on f. 10r–10v and arranged in numbered stanzas with each pair of lines written side by side, making stanzas of four 'long' lines each. It is probably a sister-manuscript to A and B, see the accounts of A, B, C, D and E on pp. 29–30 and 35–37 above and pp. 65–71 below.

There are the following distinctive readings in C:

st. 7: vistar C] vistum A, E, vistum B, vistom D
st. 8: syrga C] syrgia A, B, D, E

st. 10: hemis C] heimis A, B, D, E
st. 16: grun*n*is C] Grymis A, G*ri*mnis B, Grimnis D, E
st. 19: bekkar C] beckjar A, beckiar B, E, becciar D
st. 22: leg*g*a C] leggia A, D, E, leggia B

Four of these distinctive readings, 'syrga', 'hemis', 'bekkar' and 'legga', are secondary, and look like careless copying errors (though with the first, third and fourth cf. st. 14/6 'rygar' and commentary). The others could be attempts to improve the text where a scribe did not fully understand words or names in his original, though 'grunnis' could easily be due to a misreading of the first four minims in 'Grimnis'. C is not a copy of either A or B. C has 'þvi' in st. 3, where the whole B group has the error 'þur', and in st. 13, 'of miþgard', where the B group has 'ofǫnþg*ar*ð'. In st. 15, 'at syn v*ar* fyrir', and st. 24, 'jarkna', C has similar readings to B and D and E. In st. 1, C shares the reading 'occar'/'okkar' with D against A, B and E.

In 1841 the manuscript was examined by Jón Sigurðsson, whose description of it is in AM 927 4to (see Jón Helgason 1962–1981, III xiii). It was used by Bugge (*Norrœn fornkvæði* 1867, xlviii) in his edition of the eddic poems. Jón Helgason edited the first sixteen of the narrative poems in *Íslenzk fornkvæði* 1962–1981, III. The manuscript is described there on pp. xi–xv.

Description of D

Thott 1491 4to (D), which consists of 237 leaves, was written in the eighteenth century. It is bound in leather, and the spine originally had gold tooling. The title there, which has partly disappeared at the edges, reads '⟨S⟩ÆMUNDA⟨R⟩ | EDDA'. At the back of the manuscript a slip has been inserted on which *Hávamál* 90/3–4 is quoted, and inside has been placed a letter from Skúli Magnússon to Thott, dated Copenhagen, 2. February 1770. According to this letter, it is accompanied by the Edda ('Her med følger Edda'). Otherwise it is mainly concerned with Icelandic matters, but towards the end it reads:

> Nu vil man vende sig fra det her [the Icelandic content]: Vi vil gaae op i de utænkelige Tiider. Midt i Arbeydet om Menniskene maatte Edda her for en Dag. Den følger da her med. Hos slet ingen kand jeg deponere bedre end i Deres højgrevelig Excellences Bogsamling.

Kålund says (1900, 333) that D appears to be put together from various originally unrelated parts, but it is rather written by a single hand using alternately cursive and Gothic script.

The manuscript has as its title on f. 1r: 'Edda | Islendinga | Skrifud af Diakna Paule | efter bestu Membrana sem | Island aa'. In 966 it said that *Grottasǫngr* there was copied from a manuscript owned by Páll Sveinsson

Torfasonar (1704–1784), though he had not written it himself. Páll was a parish clerk and wrote several manuscripts, so it is probably he that is meant here. But the colophon in D on f. 203v says that the manuscript as far as *Hamðismál* was copied from one written by Síra Þórður Jónsson (1672–1720) of Staðarstaður, which was itself a copy of the Codex Regius. The manuscript opens with the Codex Regius poems in the same order, then some supplements to *Hávamál*, then *Grottasǫngr*, *Gróugaldur*, *Fjölsvinnsmál*, *Hyndluljóð* and *Hrafnagaldur* (introduced with the words 'Hæc Seqventia ex Libro qvodam Chartaceo exscripta, pertinent ad Paginam 287'). Finally there is Björn of Skarðsá's treatise on runes, which among other things contains *Sigrdrífumál*.

On f. 208v, after the supplements to *Hávamál*, there is some information about the part of the manuscript that contains the Codex Regius poems:

> Hactenus Exemplar Sal. S. Þordar Jonssonar ad Stadarstad, Profasts i Snæfells Ness Syslu, sem er med han*n*s þeckianlegu hendi af honum samanbored vid þá bestu Codices bædi Membranas og a Papyri og til settar Variantes Lectiones. Hvort Exemplar nu á S. Jon Jonsson Prestur til Flugumyrar og Hialta Stada i Skaga firde.

After *Grottasǫngr*, *Gróugaldur*, *Fjölsvinnsmál*, *Hyndluljóð* and *Hrafnagaldur* there is a note on f. 229r about the manuscript that these poems were copied from:

> Þessar fimm seinustu Qvidur, sydan Exemplar S. Þordar ad Stadar Stad hætte, eru skrifadar epter oepterrettanlegu Exscripto, sem ein*n* Vidvaningur hafde skrifad, so eg er vijda ecki viss um, hvornig eg átte ad skipta Strophir, þvi allt þad Exscriptum sem eg hafde, imo, þad epter hveriu Vidvaningurin*n* skrifad hafde, var i Sijfellu. Somuleidis var eg opt oviss i þvi hvörnig eg stafa skillde so ad rett være. Eru so þessar Qvidur einasta til þess, ad syna þad þær vantade i hid goda Exemplar Sal. Sr. Þordar Jonssonar sem fyrr er nefnt, en munu þo eiga ad koma aptan vid þad. Þo mun ecke godum Codicibus öllum saman koma um*m* Röd qvidanna.

Páll Sveinsson, who, as stated above, wrote the manuscript, says here that the five listed poems were copied from a poor original written out by a beginner. No variant readings are quoted for *Hrafnagaldur*. The poem is written in unnumbered eight-line stanzas on pp. 452–457 (ff. 226r–228v). From st. 9 inclusive it is to save space written in two columns on each page.

There are the following distinctive readings in D:

st. 2: ættom D] ætlun A, B, C, E
st. 2: voria D] veria A, C, E, ve*r*ia B
st. 3: griviar D] grunar A, C, E, gr*u*nar B
st. 6: Ivars D] Ivaldz A, Ivalds B, C, E
st. 8: vargsbelgs D] vargsbelg A, va*r*gsbelg B, vargs belg C, vargsvelg E

st. 9: heim D] heims A, B, C, E
st. 11: bondo D] banda A, B, C, E[33]
st. 14: or viþ D] ǫrvit A, B, C, oruit E
st. 15: jol mun D] jolnum A, B, jólnum C, iotnum E
st. 16: hyrþar D] hirdir A, B, hirdir C, E
st. 17: yþr D] jþar A, i þar B, iþar C, idar E
st. 18: baþiss D] baþu A, B, baþo C, badu E
st. 18: sumbla D] sumbli A, B, C, E
st. 18: yggiom D] Yggiongi A, B, E, Yggiongi C
st. 20: unorm D] undorn A, B, C, E
st. 22: Oþinn D] Omi A, Onn B, Onn C, Ome E
st. 23: varla D] valla A, B, C, E

The majority of the distinctive readings in D are secondary; they are obvious scribal errors that arose in copying. For 'varla' (st. 23), A, B, C and E have 'valla' (A also adds 'vallda' in parentheses within the stanza), which could be an orthographical variant of *varla* at this date, but might also be gen. pl. of 'vǫllur' in a kenning. Only 'varla' seems to be meaningful in the context, though even so a great deal of alteration of the word order is required (see the commentary on this stanza). St. 23 must be corrupt, so it is difficult to judge what might have stood in the archetype. Scribes might easily substitute 'varla' for its homophone 'valla' or vice versa. The distinctive reading 'Oþinn' could be primary, and like 'Omi/Ome' in A and E would fit in with the tendency in the poem for there to be four syllables in each line, unlike Onn in B and C, but, as stated above, 'Omi' is to be preferred. D does not reproduce the distinctive readings of A, B or C.

Hrafnagaldur in D must be derived from the lost common original of A, B and C. It was copied from a manuscript that was written out as prose ('i Sijfellu'), but this does not necessarily mean that it was not copied from the same original as they were (see pp. 70–71 below), but the number of errors in the text makes it seem at a greater remove from the archetype, and it may have come through several intermediate links. Its immediate source is unknown.

D was used by Jón Eiríksson in his preliminary work for the Arnamagnæan edition of the eddic poems in 47. He took variant readings from it, marked 'P.S.' [Páll Sveinsson].

DESCRIPTION OF E

Lbs 1441 4to (E), which consists of 326 leaves + 2 flyleaves bound in leather, was written c. 1760. It is in poor condition; the binding has come

---

[33] E adds in parentheses above the line 'borda'.

apart and the leaves have crumbled away at the edges and been repaired. It is a collection of eddic poems and other poems in eddic metres. On the title page (f. 1r) is written: 'Á þessa bök er skryfud EDDA Sæmundar Sigfussonar hinns froda, Sóknar prests ad Odda i Rangærvalla sijslu i Austfyrding⟨a⟩fiordunge a Islandi, ad Störu Reikium i Midfijrde 176⟨0⟩'. The manuscript is written in two hands. Most of the poems are according to the catalogue written in a hand similar to that of Guðmundur Ísfold, which has also numbered the pages. At the beginning there is a preface written by Síra Þorsteinn Pétursson of Staðarbakki, and at the end some texts are inserted written in the same hand: *Rígsþula*, *Bergbúa þáttr*, a series of arguments, *Sólarljóð*, *Hákonarmál*, *Vísa trémanns í Sámseyju* from *Ragnars saga*, stanzas by among others Egill Skallagrímsson, a series of *heiti*, *Sonatorrek* and *Hǫfuðlausn*. Finally there is a commentary on some of the poems.

On ff. 13r–20v there is a list of contents with notes on some of the poems. The order of the poems is the same as in the Codex Regius, but after *Hamðismál* there follow *Baldrs draumar*, *Heiðreks gátur*, *Hyndluljóð*, *Gróugaldur*, *Fjölsvinnsmál*, *Hrafnagaldur* (no. xxxv), *Grottasǫngr*, *Rígsþula*, *Sólarljóð*, *Hákonarmál*, *Hǫfuðlausn*, *Sonatorrek*, *Krákumál* and *Bergbúa þáttr*.

After *Grottasǫngr* Þorsteinn Pétursson has added: 'N.B. Fleire flokka f. Sæmundar Eddu hef eg hvorki heirt nie sied, Resenid [sic] telur þá alls 19, og eins vor margfródi Bp. D Finnur ecke fleire, og þvi mä þessi Bök vera hin fullkomnasta sem fäst kann ä vorum daugum. Þ.P.S.' There is no information about the source of the manuscript or of individual poems in it.

Hrafnagaldur is written on pp. 538–546 (ff. 289v–293v), and placed between *Fjölsvinnsmál* and *Grottasǫngr*. It is arranged in unnumbered eight-line stanzas. This manuscript is unique, in that it blends stt. 21 and 25 together, so that st. 25/1–2 + 5–6 follow immediately after the first half of st. 21. Then follows the second half of st. 21 and then st. 25/3–4 + 7–8. This error could have arisen during copying.

There are the following distinctive readings in E:

st. 1: skiria E] skilia A, B, C, scilia D
st. 2: veita E] viltu A, C, D, villtu B
st. 3: dulur E] dulu A, B, C, dulo D.
st. 4: faulnum E] follnum A, follnum B, follnom C, folgnom D
st. 8: vargsvelg E[34]] vargsbelg A, vargsbelg B, vargs belg C, vargsbelgs D

---

[34] Here in the margin at the bottom of the page is written in a different hand 'án efa vargsbelg'.

st. 10: ranni E] ran*n* A, B, C, rann D
st. 11: borda bruda E[35]] banda burþa A, B, C, bondo burþa D
st. 12: knattu E] knatti A, B, C, D
st. 13: mid natt E[36]] meþ natt A, B, C, D
st. 14: gylu E] glygiu A, glygio B, C, D
st. 15: Iorun E] Jormi A, B, C, D
st. 15: iotnum E] jolnum A, B, jolnu*m* C, jol mun D
st. 19: skolug E] Ska/gul A, B, Ska/gull C, Scaugul D
st. 24: men E] mǫn A, B, C, maun D
st. 26: upprann E] upp nam A, B, C, D

Many of the distinctive readings are secondary and appear to be careless mistakes that arose in copying. This applies to 'skiria', 'dulur', 'vargsvelg', 'knattu', 'borda bruda', 'gylu', 'skolug' and 'upprann'. Others could be an attempt to improve the text where a scribe did not fully understand words or names in his original. This applies to 'veita', 'ranni', 'mid natt', 'Iorun', 'iotnum' and 'men'. Of these 'veita' and 'iotnum' give unsatisfactory sense in the context. 'faulnum' in st. 4 is only a spelling variant of 'föllnum'; the verb *fella* is used in the preceding line, and the poet appears to have had a predilection for using homonymous and sometimes cognate words of differing meanings close to each other. In st. 10, 'ranni' could be a case of an alteration or correction, since *at* most often governs the dative (cf. commentary). By line 8 in st. 13, 'med natt hvor', 'mid' is written in the margin. This could be a case of alteration, and 'mid' was perhaps not in the scribe's original. Most lines in the poem moreover have four syllables, but here (in the manuscripts) there are only three. In st. 15 the other manuscripts have the unknown word (or name) 'Jormi'. E's 'Iorun' may be a case of correction, but it is also possible that it was the original reading (confusion of minims). In st. 24 the jewel-adorned chariot might have inspired the scribe to make the change to 'men', since one can imagine that the horse might have had an ornamented collar.

Since E does not reproduce any of the distinctive readings of A, B, C or D, it cannot be derived from any of them, and seems to have independent textual value. The large number of distinctive readings it contains suggests that it was derived from the archetype via several intervening copies.

---

[35] Added above the line in E in parentheses above 'banda burda'.

[36] 'mid' is added in lighter ink in the same hand in the margin where the text has 'med natt'.

Relationship of the Principal Manuscripts

A has preserved a text with fewer errors than B, C, D and E, though in a few cases these have superior readings. There are some erroneous spellings that appear in all five, which might suggest that the archetype was at least at one remove from the original, though they do not amount to much:

st. 13: 'atri'
st. 14: 'glygiu'
st. 16: 'nepa'

The original reading in st. 13 may have been 'acri' or 'hatri', since *c* and *t* can be almost identical in gothic script. 'glygiu' obviously should be 'glygvi', and the error must be due to confusion of minims. St. 16, 'nepa' for 'nefa' is no doubt due to the misunderstanding of an insular *f* (cf. commentary). These errors could all three be due to scribes independently misreading an unclear original.

B, C, D and E have no errors in common against A (except perhaps for st. 13, 'hvǫr/hvorr/hver/hvor' for 'hvǫria', see textual notes), but each of the five has its own innovations that are not shared by any of the others, and there is nothing to indicate that any of them is derived from any of the others. In st. 7, B, C and D have 'hardbaþins'/'hardbaþnis', while A has 'hardbadms' and E has 'harbadms'. In addition, C and D share the reading 'okkar'/'occar' in st. 1 against A, B and E, which have 'or*r*kar'/'orkar'. In both of these cases, the errors could easily have been made by different scribes independently of each other.

There appears to be only one shared reading between A and B against the other manuscripts: in st. 1, A has 'þiá', B has 'þia', C has 'þrá', D and E have 'þra'. The verbs *þjá* and *þrá* are virtual synonyms in this context, though the first is usually transitive, the second intransitive. This is hardly enough to suggest a common original for A and B different from that of C, D and E, though the way the poem is arranged in stanzas in the different manuscripts might support the idea. In A and B the stanzas are written out continuously as prose, with divisions between stanzas marked by paragraph breaks, and these two manuscripts both have the same mistake in stanza division in stt. 20–21, attaching the first half of st. 21 to st. 22, leaving the second half of st. 22 as a short stanza. But the information is given in D, which is written out in eight-line stanzas, that its original was not arranged in stanzas, and this may also have been the case in the archetype of all five manuscripts and perhaps also in the original poem (as was also the case in the Codex Regius). There is an example of a manuscript derived from B (21.6.7) in which the poem is not divided into stanzas, and there are others where it is written in eight-line stanzas, so it is clear that some scribes could arrange a poem written out as prose in the manuscript they were copying into stanzas, while others could change a version divided into stanzas back to one with no stanza divisions. In E, too, the poem is arranged in eight-line stanzas, and no error in the stanza divisions corresponding to that in A and B is found in either D or E, but on the other hand stt. 21 and 25 are merged together in E (see the account of this manuscript on pp. 67–69 above). This error could have arisen when the copy in E was being made, though the possibility cannot be excluded that the error was in its original, for it is hardly likely that the scribe of E corrected the error in stt. 20 and 21 and immediately afterwards introduced an error that must be due to carelessness in stt. 20 and 25. In A the scribe discovered the mistake in stt. 20 and 21and wrote a long stroke to indicate that the second half of st. 21 belonged with the previous stanza. This error in the stanza division must have existed in the common original of A and B; obviously it would have been easy enough for most scribes to have spotted it. Thus there is no error in the division of C's stanzas written in paragraphs of four lines each. The error could therefore have been in the archetype of all five manuscripts. There is no good reason to think that there is any special relationship between A and B. The similarities between them are presumably due to the fact that they both originated in Skálholt.

Establishing the five manuscript groups therefore causes no problems. A number of innovations or secondary readings are found in the individual groups that are not found in any of the other ones. None of the principal manuscripts reproduces the distinctive readings in any of the principal manuscripts of the other groups. The following stemma may therefore reflect the relationships of the manuscripts. X, the archetype, may have been identical with the 'old and dirty leaf' (pp. 12–13 above), on which the writing may have been unclear; this may even have been the author's autograph. It was perhaps written in imitation of the orthography of the Codex Regius (cf. st. 16 'nepa' for 'nefa'). This might also explain 'atri' for 'acri', the muddle over minims and other misreadings:

		X		
A	B	C	D	E

There may have been further lost links, for instance between X and D and between X and E, which both seem more remote from what must have stood in X.

Manuscripts Derived from Printed Books

A few manuscripts are derived from printed editions. This applies to ÍBR 36 4to, which is a copy of *Edda* 1787–1828, I; JS 494 8vo, a copy of Rasmus Rask's edition (1818); ÍBR 24 8vo, a copy of Hallgrímur Scheving's edition (1837); and finally Lbs 2859 4to, a copy of Bugge's edition (1867).

ÍBR 36 4to (36)

This manuscript, which was written in 1829, consists of 208 leaves. It is bound in leather, on which a design is embossed. On the flyleaf is written the title 'QVIDUR | fornar úr svokalladri | SÆMUNDAR | EDDU | Safn Sæmundar á ad enda á | Solar-Liódum | Koma þó fleiri fornqvidur inn sem eg veit ei hvört hans | Safni tilheira, enn set á Spátziunni þær eg veit. | Ritadar anno MDCCCXXIX'. After this there is a line written in runes, stating that the scribe was Einar frá Starrastöðum. This is Einar Bjarnason (1782–1856), who wrote a number of manuscripts. As the title implies, the manuscript contains eddic poems and later poems in eddic style.

On f. 2r–2v There is a list of contents. They are: *Vǫluspá, Hávamál, Vafþrúðnismál, Baldrs draumar, Þrymskviða, Hárbarðsljóð, Skírnismál, Hrafnagaldur, Hymiskviða, Lokasenna, Rígsþula, Grottasǫngr, Gróugaldur, Grímnismál, Alvíssmál, Fjölsvinnsmál, Heiðreks gátur, Helgakviða Hjǫrvarðssonar, Helgakviða Hundingsbana I, Helgakviða Hundingsbana II, Frá dauða Sinfjǫtla, Grípisspá, Reginsmál, Fáfnismál, Sigrdrífumál, Guðrúnarkviða I, Sigurðarkviða in skamma, Helreið Brynhildar, Dráp Niflunga, Guðrúnarkviða II, Oddrúnargrátr, Gunnarsslagur, Atlakviða, Atlamál in grænlenzku, Hamðismál*, stanzas from *Guðrúnarhvǫt, Vǫlundarkviða, Bjarkamál, Hyndluljóð, Krákumál, Ynglingatal, Hǫfuðlausn, Hákonarmál, Sólarljóð*. After these is added an introduction to Sæmundar Edda by Finnur Magnússon, then *Hugsvinnsmál, Merlínusspá, Háttalykill Lopts ins ríka, Nora eðr Njörva jötuns kviða, Inntak vísnanna úr Grettis sögu* and *Hellisvísur* from *Bergbúa þáttr* with comments and 'nokkur orð í Huldar sögu'.

The manuscript is written in four hands. The *Háttalykill* was written by Einar Bjarnarson. Then follows, in the same hand as wrote all the preceding poems, *Nora eðr Njörva jötuns kviða*, and finally, in the same gathering as *Nora eðr Njörva jötuns kviða*, a selection of verses from *Grettis saga* made by Jón Ólafsson, to which are added notes to some of the poems in the hand of Guðmundur Einarsson, sheriff's secretary, and some comments to stanzas of *Hellisvísur* in a further unknown hand.

Hrafnagaldur is written on pp. 67–72 (ff. 35r–37v). It is arranged in unnumbered eight-line stanzas. The text is set out as in a scholarly edition: variant apparatus is added at the foot of the page, where both variant readings and possible emendations are given. The text has some readings that appear in printed editions, for example 'illa' in st. 2, and among the possible emendations are some that are mentioned in *Edda* 1787–1828, I. In st. 2 there is the reading 'Oðhręris scyldi | urdr geima', where the manuscripts have 'Óðhrærir' in the nominative and 'Urðar' in the genitive.

Other examples confirm that 36 is a copy of the Arnamagnæan edition, since it includes emendations and readings that are only found there, for example 'verri' in st. 7, 'at ranni' in st. 10 (though see E), 'Eins oc kémr' and 'af ato' in st. 13. On a later occasion the scribe has, however, added emendations from Scheving's edition (1837): to 'hinnaleitar' in st. 3, is added 'hennar leita', and in st. 13, to 'ato' is added 'akri'; both these are taken from there.

This manuscript previously bore the numbers ÍBR A. 57, ÍBR A. 68, ÍBR A. 58.

JS 494 8vo (494)

This manuscript consists of 189 leaves, with which four additional leaves have been bound in at the front containing a title page and a list of contents. It was written at the beginning of the nineteenth century. It is the twenty-fifth volume of a collection of poems comprising fifty volumes in all (JS 470–519 8vo). It is bound in paper and cloth. On the first leaf is written: 'Þessa bók gaf mér Páll stúdent Pálsson í Reykjavík í September mánuði 1862. Jón Árnason.' On the second: 'Kvæda-safn. | XXV. | innihald. | Fyrst: nokkrar pápiska*r* bænir. | sídan: Mariu- og önnur andlig | forn-kvædi, eddu-kvædi. | o.fl. | og aptast: Lesrím Ó. Hjaltalins | ágríp af Postula-æfum | Teikn t*il* vedráttufars | etc. | Frá Registríu: | Allt med hendi Jóns Jónssonar, um tíma fyrir svars bónda á Øndverdarnesi í Snæfellsnes s., sidan á Arnarstapa, hvar hann dó í Stapabol, árid 1828.' The reference is presumably to the *ríma*-poet Jón Jónsson 'langur' (1779–1828), who lived in various places in Iceland (see *Íslenzkar Æviskrár* 1948–1976, III 196; *Rímnatal* 1966, II 89). On f. 3 there is an alphabetical list of the first words of the poems ('eptir byriun kvædanna'), and on f. 4 an alphabetical list of their titles. The first part of the manuscript contains pre-Reformation prayers and religious poems. The second part has various eddic poems: *Hugsvinnsmál, Hávamál, Vǫluspá, Vafþrúðnismál, Gróugaldur, Sólarljóð, Gunnarsslagur, Lokasenna, Hrafnagaldur, Frá dauða Sinfjǫtla* (in prose), *Þrymskviða, Baldrs draumar, Vǫlundarkviða*. The third part contains calendar calculations, and has on f. 132v the title 'Nýtt | Les-ríím | sem kien*n*er ad útreikna | Arsins adskilianlegar-Tídir | samt. | Túngl komur | og an*n*ad hier ad lútandi, | sama*nn* skrifad af O. Hialtalin, | Distrikts kírurgus og konstit: | Landphysikus. | Beitistödum 1817. | Prentad á kostnad Rithöfunds | ens | af G. Scagfiörd.' That is, the third part was copied from a printed book that was published at Beitistaðir in 1817. At the end of the manuscript two leaves from another manuscript with magical runes have been inserted.

Hrafnagaldur is in the second part of the manuscript on ff. 116v–118v (pp. 232–236) after *Lokasenna* and before *Frá dauða Sinfjǫtla* and

Hymiskviða. The stanzas are numbered, but the line breaks within the stanzas are random. The title is written in red.

The text in 494 follows emendations in Rask's edition (st. 3, 'hugen*n*', st. 20, 'huma'), that are otherwise not found in manuscripts. This applies also to 'illa' in st. 2, which also appears in the Arnamagnæan edition. It is probably a direct or indirect copy of Rask's edition. That it cannot be a copy of Scheving's edition is shown by the reading 'huma' in st. 20, where Scheving has 'hymia' or 'himia'.

ÍBR 24 8vo (24)

This manuscript, which consists of 78 leaves + 1 flyleaf, was written c. 1840. It is bound in leather, on which a design is embossed. It contains poems in eddic metres and bears the title 'Lioða Eðða | eðr | EDDA RHYTMICA | Sęmundar Sigfussonar | hinns froda | j Odda. ritud ar 1122.'

According to information written in a different hand on the flyleaf, it was written by the farmer Jón Níelsson of Grænanes (died 1842). It was given, together with ÍBR 25 and 26 8vo, to Landsbókasafn Íslands by Síra Guðmundur Gísli Sigurðsson, who had got it from the scribe's son, Jóhann. On f. 78v after the final poem is written: 'Endir Drápunar hvöria þiodolfr orti um*m* Rögnvald heidum hærra. *ok* prentut er i Heimskringla. Stadfestir ritarinn'. Underneath is added the name 'G. G. Sigurdsson Níelsson', and under that 'Edda, Jóhann Jónsson á bokína og féck hana i sínn födur Arf 1848'. On the title page is written 'G. G. Sigurðsson' and in the top right hand corner the initials 'G. G. S.'

On the verso of the flyleaf there is a list of contents: 'Innihald Eddu þessarar'. The poems are *Hrafnagaldur, Vǫluspá, Vafþrúðnismál, Grímnismál, Skírnismál, Hávamál, Hárbarðsljóð, Hymiskviða, Lokasenna, Þrymskviða, Alvíssmál, Vǫlundarkviða, Helgakviða Hundingsbana I, Helgakviða Hjǫrvarðssonar, Helgakviða Hundingsbana II, Sólarljóð, Guðrúnarkviða I, Sigrdrífumál, Rúnadeilur, Gunnarsslagur, Brísingamen, Hugsvinnsmál* and parts of *Sigrdrífumál*. At the end are written 'Viðbætir Eddu', among other things genealogies, *Fundinn Noregr* and *Ynglinga drápa*.

Hrafnagaldur is arranged in numbered eight-line stanzas on ff. 2r–3v. After it is written in a different hand: 'Nyjari fornfræðingar (P. A. Munck) telja kvæði þetta miklu yngra enn Völuspá, og þykir það ærið torskilið. Dr. Schéving hefur gefið það út í Viðey 1832 [sic]'.

Hrafnagaldur in 24 has readings and emendations that were introduced into the printed editions of the poem. Some of these are only found in Scheving's edition (1837), so *Hrafnagaldur* in this manuscript must be a copy of that. There are examples in st. 3, 'hen*n*ar leita', 'er dvelr', 'þótta

þráins', 'draumr þótta', st. 11, 'vörþr', st. 21, 'oc lítil fræga' and st. 24, 'járna steinum'.
This manuscript previously bore the number ÍBR B. 1.

Lbs 2859 4to (2859)
This manuscript, which was written by Jón A. Hjaltalín in 1870, has 201 leaves. It is a large volume in quarto format, finely bound in red leather with gilt tooling on both binding and paper. On f. 1r stands the title 'Sæmundar Edda | Part second | with | an English Translation and Notes | by | Jón A. Hjaltalín. | London 1870.' The spine bears the similar title 'Saemundar Edda | Part II. | With Translation | Jón A. Hjaltalín'.

According to the catalogue the manuscript came to Landsbókasafn Íslands in 1944 from Dr Grace Thornton, who had studied Icelandic and in the 1940s was head of the Scandinavian department at the Ministry of Information in London and for a time was employed as press attaché and information officer with the British Embassy in Denmark.

2859 is the second part of a collection of eddic poems and poems in eddic style. It contains first the heroic poems in the usual order. After *Hamðismál* follow *Grottasǫngr*, *Grougaldur*, *Fjölsvinnsmál*, *Sólarljóð* and last of all *Hrafnagaldur* (as poem no. 25, on ff. 197r–201v).

Each poem is accompanied by extensive notes at the bottom of each page. *Hrafnagaldur* is introduced by the following words, which are reminiscent of Bugge's verdict on the poem in 1867, just a few years before Hjaltalín wrote this manuscript:

> There is no doubt that this song is nothing but an imitation of the genuine Edda-songs, composed by a poet living probably in the sixteenth or the seventeenth, century. Unlike the genuine Edda-songs it was not handed down through oral tradition from one generation to another, but was committed to writing as soon as it issued from the brain of the author ... Therefore I endorse without the least hesitation the suggestion of <u>Bugge</u> that this poem ought to be excluded from the <u>Edda</u>.

2859 is the latest known manuscript to contain *Hrafnagaldur*. After originally having taken a distinguished place among the earliest and therefore the most important poems, *Hrafnagaldur* has now, thanks to Hjaltalín's introduction and its physical placing at the end of the manuscript, been degraded. As a literary and learned product, it is now regarded as a spurious eddic poem.

Hrafnagaldur in 2859 has several readings derived from the printed editions, for example, st. 2, 'máttk at', st. 7, 'hárbaðms', st. 20, 'húma', and st. 23, 'fóðrlarðr', so it must be taken from one of these. Some of its readings are only found in Bugge's edition, so that must be its source. As examples can be mentioned st. 21, 'oflítilfræga' and st. 26, 'upp nam ár Gjöll'. In 2859 Hjaltalín also uses the titles *Svipdagsmál I* and *Svipdagsmál II*, which were introduced by Bugge, for the poems that in most manuscripts are called *Grógaldur* and *Fjölsvinnsmál*.

OTHER MANUSCRIPTS

KB Add 14 4to (14)
This manuscript contains Latin translations of *Hrafnagaldur* and *Hávamál* with a commentary in Latin to *Hávamál*. In addition it has word lists to various eddic poems. It consists of twelve leaves written in the second half of the eighteenth century by Jón Eiríksson, chief librarian in Det kongelige Bibliotek, Copenhagen, who also wrote 47. It is bound, and f. 12 is blank.

The translation of *Hrafnagaldur* is on ff. 1r–2r. It is derived from the translation begun by Helgi Ólafsson, but some changes have been made compared with the translations in both 34 and 1870 (in st. 1), while it shares some of the changes in 1870 compared with 34 (in stt. 24 and 25). It is therefore likely that the translation in 14 is a copy of that in 1870 with some changes. It is not the same as Guðmundur Magnússon's translation in *Edda* 1787–1828, I.

AM 424 fol. (424)
This contains Gunnar Pálsson's autograph commentary to *Hárbarðsljóð*, *Hymiskviða*, *Lokasenna*, *Baldrs draumar* and *Hrafnagaldur* and to verses in *Gunnlaugs saga*. It is a paper manuscript with 100 leaves from the eighteenth century which earlier bore the catalogue number Addit. 25, fol. in the University Library, Copenhagen. The commentaries, which Gunnar sent to Copenhagen in 1779, had been requested by the Arnamagnæan Commission, which considered help from Iceland for the interpretation of the eddic poems a necessity. Gunnar enjoyed high regard as one of the best interpreters of the *Edda* (see Finnur Jónsson 1930, 229–231).

Gunnar's commentary on *Hrafnagaldur*, which is on ff. 48r–53v, was used by Guðmundur Magnússon in *Edda* 1787–1828, I. The manuscript was also used and described in *Íslendinga sögur* 1843–1847, II xxx.

LOST MANUSCRIPTS

Already by 1650 there existed several copies of the eddic poems, and in the course of the second half of the seventeenth century and the eighteenth century numerous collections of eddic poetry were turned out. Demand for these manuscripts was very high, as the above account of the manuscripts shows. Árni Magnússon possessed a number of manuscripts of eddic poems; no fewer than fifteen collections he owned were destroyed in the fire in 1728 (see *Norrœn fornkvæði* 1867, lxii). In his letter to Jón Halldórsson (discussed on pp. 11–12 above), Árni says that he had owned two manuscripts written by Þorsteinn Eyjólfsson that had both contained eddic poems, and among these *Hrafnagaldur*. These were both destroyed in 1728.

It is known that Árni Magnússon had possessed at least one other text of *Hrafnagaldur*. The poem was in AM 582 4to when he acquired it in Iceland in 1710. That manuscript now contains riddarasögur and fornaldarsögur, but according to a note on the flyleaf, Árni removed two texts from it: 'Hier var og i Hrafnagalldur Ódins og Dissertatiuncula de origine vocis væringiar, sem eg tok hier frá'. The note is not in Árni's hand, it was written by an amanuensis at his dictation. This text of *Hrafnagaldur* is apparently lost (see Jensen 1983, lxxxviii).

A number of texts of *Hrafnagaldur* that are mentioned in the existing manuscripts seem to have perished. Magnús Jónsson of Vigur in Ísafjarðardjúp wrote one that cannot be identified among the surviving manuscripts, though a copy survives of it in 21.6.7 made by Jón Egilsson, farmer at Stóra-Vatnshorn. In the surviving manuscripts containing *Hrafnagaldur* we also read that Bjarni Halldórsson and Eyjólfur Jónsson possessed manuscripts containing collections of eddic poems, but Eyjólfur Jónsson's at any rate did not include *Hrafnagaldur*. In 1109, Jón Ólafsson, vice lawman at Eyri in Seyðisfjörður, states that this manuscript had been copied from a manuscript collated with several paper manuscripts and an 'ypperlig' codex that Eyjólfur Jónsson, priest at Vellir in Svarfaðardalur, had written. 1109 is derived from a manuscript belonging to Jón Egilsson, once vice-principal at Hólar and later priest at Laufás. Neither Eyjólfur's nor Jón's manuscript seems to have survived.

Halldór Hjálmarsson states in a note about the source of 1588 a I that it was a copy of a manuscript written by Po. H. S. This may refer to Páll Hjálmarsson, who was Halldór's brother (see Verri 2007, 28).

Páll Sveinsson states in D that he has copied *Hrafnagaldur* (and four other poems) from a manuscript, written by a beginner. According to Páll, that text was written out continuously as prose. None of the surviving manuscripts answers to this description, so we may assume that the manuscript is lost.

Gunnar Pálsson, who wrote a commentary to *Hrafnagaldur*, also owned a manuscript of the poem, in which Páll Vídalín had written by the title: 'það er Forspiallslióð'. None of the known manuscripts of *Hrafnagaldur* contains such a remark, so this manuscript too is probably lost.

Finally, in the Arnamagnæan edition a manuscript belonging to Geir Vídalín was used that cannot be identified with any surviving manuscript, since in Guðmundur Magnússon's variant apparatus readings are quoted from it (marked 'G.') that cannot be found in any existing manuscript. So they cannot even be used to determine the position of Geir's manuscript in the stemma. It has as far as possible been attempted to fit the lost manuscripts into the stemma of the B group, but it has not always been feasible.

SIGNIFICANCE OF THE MANUSCRIPT TRANSMISSION FOR THE RECEPTION OF EDDIC POEMS

The many manuscripts containing collections of eddic poems are testimony to the antiquarian interest in the eddic poems in Iceland, Denmark and Sweden. This antiquarian activity, which took place primarily in the seventeenth and eighteenth centuries, is to a large extent not appreciated today. From the time that eddic poems first came to be known about, in 1643, learned Icelanders began to produce manuscripts that either remain in Iceland today or were presented or sold to philologists and historians in Denmark and Sweden. Rather later in the seventeenth century, interest in the eddic poems began to spread outside Scandinavia. In 1772 the British botanist Sir Joseph Banks (1743–1820) travelled to Iceland to collect plants, but he also bought manuscripts, among others one of these manuscripts of eddic poems, which ended up in the British Library. In the nineteenth century Finnur Magnússon sold a number of manuscripts (amongst others, some of the Edda) to libraries in Great Britain, and at least one reached Germany in this period.

The physical appearance of the manuscripts bears witness to the variety of social contexts in which they were found and the prestige that in some cases was accorded to them. While in Denmark some sumptuous folios, bound and ornamented with gold, are preserved, that have belonged to some of the country's most notable men, among others B. W. Luxdorph (1716–1788), P. F. Suhm (1728–1798) and Count Otto Thott (1703–1785). On the other hand, most of the manuscripts that are preserved in Iceland are in quarto, and as a result of heavy use, wear and tear and poor preservation, are in a sorry state, unbound and fragmentary. The sumptuous folios show how highly regarded the eddic poems were among those with antiquarian interests in the seventeenth and eighteenth centuries. Every antiquarian in the eighteenth century would probably have wished to have a volume of this kind standing among his books. In the production of manuscripts for Danish antiquarian's collections, paper was not spared. It is significant that today not a single one of these prestigious folios from the eighteenth century is preserved in Iceland. This indicates that the interest in Sæmund's

Edda in Iceland was among less wealthy circles than in Denmark and Sweden, among priests, poets and scholars, while in other countries scholars and antiquarians were more often influential and wealthy men. Count Otto Thott, P. F. Suhm and B. W. Luxdorph all owned collections of eddic poems in copies that had been made in Iceland. Icelandic scholars like Páll Vídalín and Gunnar Pálsson were also interested in the eddic poems and possessed copies of the so-called Sæmundar eddur. From notes in some manuscripts of *Hrafnagaldur* we also see that Eyjólfur Jónsson, priest at Vellir, and Jón Egilsson, vice-principal of the school at Hólar, possessed manuscripts containing eddic poems. Árni Magnússon's mention in his letter (see p. 12) of the copying activity in Skálholt in the time of Brynjólfur Sveinsson and Ólafur Jónsson is a testimony to the interest in the Edda early on. Notes in manuscripts reveal how people were apparently continually hunting for the best collections of eddic poems in Iceland. Thus Bishop Hersleb (1689–1757) in a longish note in NKS 1866 4to, stresses that no more than two or three copies of the same collection of eddic poems could be found in the whole of Iceland. Árni Magnússon, too, was interested in the eddic poems. It was thought in the seventeenth century that the collection of these poems had been made by Sæmundr fróði Sigfússon,[37] and according to a folktale he was supposed to have composed *Sólarljóð* himself (see note 9 above), though Árni Magnússon argued convincingly against the idea that he could have been the author. Árni's interest in the eddic poems must have been motivated by among other things his research into Sæmundr fróði, which first appeared in print after his death in *Edda* 1787–1828, I. At the time of the fire in Copenhagen in 1728 he possessed — and lost — fifteen manuscripts that contained eddic poems (see *Norræn fornkvæði* 1867, lxii), among them at least one that contained *Hrafnagaldur*.

It was for political reasons more difficult for Swedish scholars to get hold of collections of eddic poems, which is probably why there was more copying activity taking place in Sweden than in Denmark. In 1685 it was at the suggestion of Thomas Bartholin the Younger forbidden to sell manuscripts from Iceland to Swedes. The first manuscript containing *Hrafnagaldur* to reach Sweden (A) was brought there by Guðmundur Ólafsson in 1681 and sold to Antikvitetskollegiet, and this was copied several times. Copies were also made of these copies, but no copies derived from any other manuscript containing *Hrafnagaldur* than A have ever been found in Sweden. One of the manuscripts derived from A, NKS

---

[37] The earliest mention of Sæmundr fróði as a collector of eddic poems is in Jón lærði Guðmundsson's *Grænlandsannáll* from 1623 (Einar G. Pétursson 1998, 415).

1870 4to (1870), reached Copenhagen, and is, as far as is known, the only one outside Sweden. All the manuscripts in the A group, therefore, were linked to the circle of antiquarians in Sweden, where, with just the one exception, they have always remained.

The manuscripts that were written in Iceland and sent from there to Denmark and other places are a much more varied lot than the manuscripts in Sweden. The relationship of the manuscripts in the B group to B is much more complicated than the relationship of the A group manuscripts to A. Some B group manuscripts contain readings from more than one manuscript in the same group, sometimes corrections have been made, and there is a number of manuscripts that have perished. The Icelandic transmission of *Hrafnagaldur* is both more prolific and more chaotic.

The manuscripts show how the reception of *Hrafnagaldur* changed with time. Scribes and those who commissioned their work obviously strove to create ever more 'complete' collections of eddic poems, which would not only include the poems in the Codex Regius, but also poems like for example *Sólarljóð*, *Hyndluljóð*, *Baldrs draumar*, *Heiðreks gátur* and *Hrafnagaldur*. The attitude in the seventeenth and eighteenth centuries seems to have been that a good collection should include all known poems in eddic metres whether or not they had been preserved in the Codex Regius. In the earliest copies made in this period *Hrafnagaldur* has a prominent position near the beginning of the collection, between *Sólarljóð* and *Vǫluspá*. *Sólarljóð* normally came first, as said above, probably because it was believed at the time that Sæmundr fróði had composed it. *Hrafnagaldur* was probably placed next because originally it was thought to provide a kind of introductory poem to the eddic poems as a whole, and a prelude to Ragnarǫk, which was described in the next poem, *Vǫluspá*. In the course of time *Hrafnagaldur* was moved towards the end of manuscripts, as in the manuscripts in Copenhagen, where it stands alongside other poems that were not in the Codex Regius.[38]

After the appearance of the Arnamagnæan edition in 1787, copying of compilations of eddic poems continued, but now to a lesser extent. In Iceland in the nineteenth century, we see a new kind of scribal activity or

---

[38] Bugge, in his edition of the eddic poems, supported Gunnar Pálsson's theory that *Hrafnagaldur* had been composed as an introduction to *Baldrs draumar*, into which several stanzas had been interpolated (*Norrœn fornkvæði* 1867, 140). Einar G. Pétursson in a recent article has pointed out (2007, 150) 'If Bugge's guess were correct, we would expect the two poems to appear side by side in manuscripts'. *Hrafnagaldur* is not written in front of *Baldrs draumar* in the earliest manuscripts.

a different attitude to compilation, in that there come to be examples of anthologies of a more varied content than had appeared before. We also find copies of the Arnamagnæan edition, and also of Rask's and Scheving's editions, and the latest manuscript is a copy of Bugge's edition with an English translation. Here *Hrafnagaldur* is regarded as an inauthentic eddic poem, with a reference to Bugge's arguments that it ought in future to be omitted from collections of eddic poems.

TREATMENT OF THE TEXT

The transcription of the text retains the spelling of the manuscript, but capitals are used only (and always) in proper names and at the beginning of sentences. The punctuation is editorial, designed to facilitate the understanding of the poem. Abbreviations are expanded and indicated by the use of italics. The expansions are spelt in accordance with the majority spellings of the same sounds when written out in full. Thus the sign ² is transcribed as *-ur*, since the svarabhakti vowel is written in 90% of the cases where the ending is written out in full, and the sign ⁷ is transcribed *-ir*, since that is the spelling in 92% of the cases where this ending is written out in full. Superscript letters are treated as abbreviations.

Emendations are marked by an asterisk. Illegible letters or words are supplied in pointed brackets ⟨ ⟩.

Variant readings are quoted from B, C, D and E. On one occasion a reading is quoted from 11, although it is derived from A, because it has a reading that seems to be an intentional correction by the scribe. Variants are transcribed according to the same principles as the text.

Each stanza is followed by textual notes (if any), the text printed in normalised (modern) spelling and prose word order, and a translation.

Hrafna Gal|dur Oþins For|spialls Liod

1. Alfoþr or*r*kar,
   alfar skilia,
   Vanir vitu,
   visa nornir,
   elur Iviþia,
   ald*ir* bera,
   þreya þussar,
   þia valkyriur.

Title: Hrafna] Rafna, C   1: or*r*kar] okkar, C; occar, D   2: skilia] skiria, E   3: vitu] vita, D   4: nornir] normr, B   5: Iviþia] i viþia, B   7: þussar] þursar C, D; þurs*ar*, B   8: þia] þrá, C. þra, D, E

Alföður orkar, álfar skilja, Vanir vitu, vísa nornir, elur Íviðja, aldir bera, þreyja þursar, þjá valkyrjur.

All-father exerts power, elves understand, Vanir know, norns show, Íviðja (a trollwife) strives, humans bear, giants endure, valkyries are distressed.

2. Ætlun Æsir
   alla gátu,
   verp*ir* viltu
   vęttar rúnum.
   Oðhrærer skylde
   Urdar gejma,
   mattkat veria
   mest-um þo*rr*a.

1: Ætlun] Ættom, D   Æsir] Esir, C   2: alla] *emended to* illa *in Edda 1787–1828*
4: vęttar] veita, E   7: mattkat] mattikat, E   veria] voria, D   8: mest-um] mestum, C; mest um*m*, B; mest um E

Æsir gátu alla ætlun, verpir villtu vættar rúnum. Óðhrærir skyldi Urðar geyma, máttkat verja mestum þorra.

[But] the Æsir divined the whole plan, the unpredictable ones caused muddle with the god's runes (or secrets). Óðhrærir had to look after Urður (fate), he could not protect [her] from the greater part [of the plan].

8v 3. Hverfur því hug*ur*,
hin*n*a leytar,
grunar guma
grand, ef dvelur;
þotti er *Þrains
þunga dra/m*ur*,
Daens dulu
dra/m*ur* þotti.

1: því] þur, B   3: grunar] griviar, D   5: *Þrains] *So* B; Þranis A, D; Þránis C; Þraens E   7: dulu] dulur, E

Hverfur því hugur, leitar hinna, guma grunar grand, ef [hann] dvelur; Þráins þótti er þungadraumur, þótti Dáins duludraumur.

Therefore his courage fails, he looks for the others, the people (dwarves?) suspect harm if he delays; Þráinn's thought is [filled with] a weighty dream, Dáinn's thought [with] a deceitful dream.

4. Dug*ir* með dverg*um*.
Dvina heim*ar*,
ni*þur* at Gin*n*ungs
niþi sa/kva;
opt Alsviþ*ur*
ofan*n* fellir,
opt of folln*um*
aptur safnar.

4: niþi] niþir, B, D; nidir, E   7: folln*um*] folgnom, D; faulnum, E

Dugir með dvergum. Heimar dvína, sökkva niður að Ginnungs niði; oft Alsviður fellir ofan, [og hann] oft aftur föllnum of safnar.

That's enough of the dwarves. Worlds dwindle away, they sink down to the darkness of Ginnungur. Alsviður (Óðinn?) often fells from above and often gathers up the fallen again.

5. Stend*ur* ęva
strind ne ra/þull,
lopte meþ lęvi
linnir ei stra/mi;
męrum dylst i
Mimis brun*n*e
vissa v*er*a;
vitiþ en*n* eþa hvaþ?

Strind né röðull æva stendur, lofti með lævi linnir ei straumi; vissa vera dylst í mærum brunni Mímis; vitið enn eða hvað?

Neither earth nor sun stand for ever, air with its poison does not cease [to flow] in a stream; the wise being hides itself in Mímir's renowned spring; do you understand yet, or what?

6. Dvelur i dolum
dys forvitin*n*,
Yggdrasils fra
aski hnigin*n*,
alfa ętt*ar*.
Iþune hetu
Ivaldz ellri
yngsta barna.

6: Iþune] i dune, B; Idune, C; Iduni, E   7: Ivaldz] Ivars, D

Forvitin dís, álfa ættar, hnigin frá aski Yggdrasils, dvelur í dölum; eldri barna Ivalds hétu yngsta Iðunni.

The enquiring goddess, descended from dwarves, sunk down from the ash Yggdrasill, stays in the valleys. The elder ones of the children of Ívaldur called the youngest Iðunn.

7. Eyrde illa
   ofan*n* komu,
   hardbaþms undir
   haldin meiþi;
   kun*n*e sist at
   kund*ar* Nǫrva,
   vǫn at vęri
   vistum heima.

3: hardbaþms] hardbaþins, B; hardbaþnis, C; harþbaþnis, D; harbadms, E   undir] miðir, B   4: haldin] halldinn, E   5: kun*n*e] kunnu, E   8: vistum] vistar, C

Haldin undir meiði harðbaðms, eirði [hún] illa ofankomu; vön að værri vistum heima, kunni [hún] síst að kundar Nörva (= Nótt).

Held beneath the hard tree's branch, she was unhappy with her coming down; accustomed to pleasanter lodging at home, she was least of all pleased at Nörvi's son's (night's) dwelling.

8. Sia sigtivar
   syrgia na*/*nnu
   viggiar at veom;
   vargsbelg seldu,
   let ifęr*az*,
   lyndi breytti,
   lek at lęvisi,
   lit*um* skipte.

2: syrgia] syrga, C; na*/*nnu] naumu, B; naumo, D; naun*n*o, C   4: vargsbelg] vargsbelgs, D; vargsvelg, E

Sigtívar sjá nönnu syrgja að véum viggjar (= Yggdrasill); [þeir] seldu [henni] vargsbelg, [hún] lét í færast, breytti lyndi, lék að lævísi, skipti litum.

The victory-gods (or battle-gods) see the lady grieve by the horse's dwelling/sanctuary (= Yggdrasill); they gave her a wolf's hide, she let herself be clothed in it, changed her nature, played with mischief, changed her shape.

9. Valde Viþrir
   va/rd Bifrastar
   Giallar sunnu
   gátt at fretta,
   heims hvivetna
   hvǫrt er vissi;
   Bragi ok Loptur
   báru kviþu.

3: sunnu] sumni, B   5: heims] heim, D   6: hvǫrt] hvert, C, D; hvort, E

Viðrir valdi vörð Bifrastar að frétta gátt sunnu Gjallar hvort er vissi hvívetna heims; Bragi og Loftur báru kvíðu.

Viðrir (Óðinn) chose Bifröst's guardian (Heimdallur) to ask the doorpost of the sun of Gjöll (= woman) whether she knew anything at all about the world; Bragi and Loftur (Loki) were filled with apprehension.

10. Galdur golu,
    ga/ndum riþu
    Rognir ok reiginn
    at rann heimis;
    hlustar Oþinn
    Hlidskialfi i,
    let bra/t vera
    langa vegu.

3: reiginn] reginn, B; regin, C, E   4: rann] ranni, E   heimis] hemis, C   5: Oþinn] Oþin, C; Oden, E   6: Hlidskialfi] hliþsciálfi, D, hlidskialfo, E

Rögnir og regin gólu galdur, riðu göndum að rann heimis; Óðinn hlustar í Hliðskjálfi, lét braut vera langa vegu.

Rögnir (Óðinn) and the gods chanted spells, rode on magic poles to the dwelling place (or roof) of the world; Óðinn listens in Hliðskjálf, he said the route was a long journey.

11. Frá en*n* vitri
veiga selio
banda burþa
ok bra*u*ta sin*n*a,
Hlyrnis, Heliar,
heimz, ef vissi
artid, ęfi,
aldurtila.

3: banda] bondo, D, borda, E (*added above the line in brackets*)   burþa] bruda, E (*in brackets above the line*)

Hinn vitri frá selju veiga burða banda og brauta sinna, ef [hún] vissi ártíð, ævi, aldurtila Hlýrnis, Heljar, heims.

The wise one asked the server of drinks (woman) about the gods' ancestry/offspring and their own paths, if she knew heaven's, Hel's, the world's date of death, life, end.

12. Ne mun męlti,
ne mál knatti
givo*m* greiþa,
ne gla*u*m hialde;
tar af tindust
ta*u*rgum hiarn*ar*,
eliun feldin
end*ur* rioþa.

1: Ne mun] Nemun, C   2: knatti] knattu, E   6: ta*u*rgum] torgum, E   7: feldin] feldm, B, C; falden, E

Ne mælti [hún] mun, ne knátti greiða gífum mál, ne hjaldi glaum; tár tíndust af törgum hjarnar, endurrjóða eljunfeldinn.

She spoke not her mind, she did not grant the greedy(?) ones words, she did not chat about merrymaking; tears dripped from her skull-shields (eyes), they make the energy-cloaks (eyelids) red again.

13. Eins kiem*ur* a*ı*stan*n*
ur Elivag*um*
þorn af *acri
þurs hrimkalda
hveim drep*ur* drött-e⟨r⟩
Daen allar
mę*ran* of Miþgard
meþ natt hvǫr*ia*.

3: þorn] þarn, D   *acri] atri, A, B, C, D; atre, E   5: drep*ur*] drępr, C   drött-er] *The final* r *appears to have been written as an alteration over another letter in* A; drott er, C; drottir, D; drotter, B, E   7: mę*ran*] mǫran, D   of Miþgard] ofǫnþg*ar*ð, B   8: meþ] mid, E (*in the margin*)   hvǫr*ia*] hvǫr, B; hvorr, C; hver, D; hvor, E. In A there seems to be an anomalous abbreviation mark to indicate the ending, which was perhaps in the archetype but omitted by the scribes of the other manuscripts because they could not interpret it

Eins kemur austan úr Élivogum þorn af akri þurs hrímkalda, með hveim Dáinn drepur dróttir allar nótt hverja of mæran Miðgarð.

In the same way there comes from the east out of Élivogar a thorn from the rime-cold giant's cornfield with which Dáinn pricks all people every night over all Miðgarður.

14. Dofna þa dáþ*ir*,
detta hend*ur*,
svif*ur* of svimi
sverþ Ass hvita,
ren*n*ir ǫrvit
rygar *glygvi,
sefa sveiflum
sokn giǫrvallri.

5: ǫrvit] ǫr viþ, D   6: rygar] *So* A, B, C, E; rigar, D; rygiar, 11. A*s* 11 *is derived from* A, *this is presumably a correction made by the scribe of* 11   *glygvi] glygiu, A; glygio, B, C, D; gylu, E. *The error in* ABCD *is presumably due to the misreading of the three minims in* -vi *as* iu (= ju)   7: sefa] sefi, D

Þá dofna dáðir, hendur detta, svimi svífur of sverð Áss hvíta; örvit rennir glyggvi rýgjar, [þau] sefa sveiflum sókn gjörvallri.

Then deeds become sluggish, hands fall idle, stupor hovers over the white god's sword (over the head); insensibility flows into the trollwife's wind (into the mind), these things calm in waves the whole parish.

15. Jamt þotti *Iorun
jolnum kominn
sollinn sutum,
svars er ei gátu;
*soktu þvi meir
ad *syn *var fyrir,
mun þo miþur
mę̨lgi dygþi.

1: *Iorun] *so* E; Jormi, A, B, C, D   2: jolnum] jol mun, D; iotnum, E   5: *soktu] *So* B, E; sokte, A; sokto, C, D   meir] mę̨ir, C   6: *syn *var] þeckia A (*added in the margin*)   ad *syn *var fyrir] at syn var fyrir, B; at syn var fyrer, C; at syn var fyrir, D; ad syn var fyrir, E

Jafnt þótti jólnum Jórunn komin, sútum sollin, er ei gátu svars; sóttu því meir að syn var fyrir; mælgi dyggði þó mun miður.

Just so seemed Jórunn to the gods to be affected, swollen with sorrows, when they could not get a reply; they sought the more in that they were faced with refusal; a lot of talking, however, helped much less.

16. For frumqva/dull
fregnar bra/ta,
hirdir at Herians
horni Giallar,
Nalar *nefa
nam til fylgiss;
greppur *Grimnis
grund vardveitti.

3: hirdir] hyrþar, D   at] t *altered from another letter,* A; at, B, C, D, E   5: *nefa] nepa, A, B, C, D, E   7: *Grimnis] *So* D, E; Grimnis, B; grunnis, C; Grymis, A

Frumkvöðull fregnar, hirðir að Gjallarhorni Herjans, fór brauta; nam Nálar nefa til fylgis; greppur Grímnis varðveitti grund.

The originator of the questioning, the keeper of Herjan's (Óðinn's) Gjallarhorn (Heimdallur), went on his way; he took as his companion Nál's kinsman (Loki); Grímnir's (Óðinn's) poet (the god Bragi) looked after the woman.

17. Vingolf toko
Viþars þegn*ar*,
Forniotz sefum
fluttir báþir;
jþar ganga
Æsi kveþia
Yggiar þeg*ar*
viþ aulteite.

5: jþar] i þar, B; yþr, D; idar, E   ganga] gango, D

Þegnar Viðars, fluttir báðir sefum Fornjóts, tóku Vingólf; ganga þar í, kveðja Æsi þegar við ölteiti Yggjar.

Viðar's (Óðinn's?) men, both conveyed by Fornjótur's kinsmen (winds), reached Vingólf; they go in there, greet the Æsir straight away at Yggur's (Óðinn's) merry drinking feast.

18. Heilan Hangaty
hepnastan*n* Ása
virt ǫndveigis,
vallda baþu,
sęla at sumbli
sitia dia,
ę meþ Yggiongi
yndi halda.

3: virt] vird, E   ǫndveigis] aunþvegis, D   4: baþu] baþiss, D   5: sumbli] sumbla, D   7: Yggiongi] yggiom, D

[Þeir] báðu heilan Hangatý, heppnastan Ása, valda virt öndvegis, día sitja sæla að sumbli, æ yndi halda með Yggjungi.

They wished Hangatýr (Óðinn), the most fortunate of gods, happiness as he ruled over the high seat ale, [they wished] the gods good luck as they sat at the feast, forever to enjoy pleasure with Yggjungur (Óðinn).

19. Beckjar sett
    *at Ba/lverks raþi,
    siot Sęhrimni
    saddist rakna;
    Ska/gul at skutlum
    skapt ker Hnikars
    mat af miþi
    min*n*is ho*r*num.

1: Beckjar] Bekkar, C   2: *at] *So* B, C, D, E; er, A   Ba/lverks] Bolverks, C, E
5: Ska/gul] Ska/gull, C; skolug, E   6: skapt ker] skaptk*er*, B; skaptker, C, E   8: min*n*is] Mimis, B

Sjót ragna, bekkjarsett að Bölverks ráði, saddist Sæhrímni; Skögul mat skaftker Hnikars af miði að skutlum minnishornum.

The gods' host, seated in accordance with Bölverkur's orders, were replete with Sæhrímnir (meat from the boar Sæhrímnir); Skögul meted out Hnikar's vat with mead onto trays in toast horns.

20. Margs of fragu
    maltid yf*ir*
    Heimdall ha goþ,
    ha/rgar Loka,
    spar eþa spakmal
    sprund ef kiende,
    undorn ofram*m*
    unz nam *huma.

3: ha goþ] hágoþ, C   4: ha/rgar] hǫrgar, C; horgar, E   5: spakmal] spakmál, C; spacmal, D   7: undorn] unorm, D   8: unz] uns, E   *huma] himia, A, B; hin*n*a, C; hinna, D, E

Hágoð of frágu Heimdall, hörgar [of frágu] Loka margs yfir máltíð undorn ofram [= umfram] uns nam húma, ef sprund kendi spár eða spakmál.

The high gods asked Heimdallur, the holy ones asked Loki many things over the meal on after mid-afternoon until it grew dark, about whether the woman had imparted any prophecy or wise sayings.

21. Illa letu
ordid hafa
erindis leysu
oflitil fręga;
vant at vęla
verþa mynde,
svo af svanna
svars ofgęti.

1–4: *Stanza 21 follows st. 20 in* A *without a break as far as* fręga, *where a long stroke indicates that an error has been made*; Margs of fragu – fręga *is also written as a single stanza in* B   3: erindis leysu] eyrindis leyso, C; erinþis leysa, D; eirendisleisu, E   4: oflitil fręga] of litilfręga, B   5: vant at] vantat, D   7: svanna] vana, E

[Þeir] létu erindisleysu orðið hafa illa, oflítilfræga; vant myndi verða að væla svo svars of gæti af svanna.

They said their fruitless errand had turned out badly, too little glorious; it would be hard to engineer it so that an answer would be got from the lady.

10r   22.   Ansar Omi,
allir hlyddu:
'Nott sk*al* nema
nyręþa til,
hugsi til myrgins
hv*er* sem orkar
raþ til leggia
ra*v*snar Asum.'

1: Omi] Onn, B; On*n*, C; Oþinn, D; Ome, E   5: myrgins] myrgis, E   6: hv*er*] hvor, E   7: leggia] legga, C

Ómi ansar, allir hlýddu: 'Nótt skal nema til nýræða, hugsi til morguns hver sem orkar leggja ráð Ásum til rausnar.'

Ómi (Óðinn) replies, they all listened: 'Night shall be used for new counsels, let him ponder until morning whoever labours to propose plans to the glory of the gods.'

23. Ran*n* meþ ra/stum
    Rindar moþir,
    fa/þ*ur* lardur
    Fenris valla
    gengo fra gilde;
    goþin*n* kvoddu
    Hropt ok Fryg*g*,
    sem Hrimfaxa for.

2: moþir] mosar, B; moþr, D; moder, E   3: fa/þ*ur* lardur] förular dúr, E *added in margin*   lardur] jarþar *added in the margin* A; larðr, B; lardr C; larþr, D   4: valla] varla, D; *in* A, vallda *is added in the text in brackets*

Móðir Rindar rann með röstum, föður Fenris varla larður, [þau] gengu frá gildi; goðin kvöddu Hropt og Frigg, sem fór Hrímfaxa.

The mother of Rind ran with long strides, [she and] the scarcely tired father of Fenrir (Loki) left the feast; the deities said farewell to Hroptur (Óðinn) and Frigg, who went with Hrímfaxi (night).

24. Dyr*um* settan*n*
    Dellings ma/g*ur*
    jo fram*m*keyrþi
    *jarkna stein*um*;
    mars of manheim
    mǫn af glo*ar*
    dro leik Dvalins
    dra/sull i reiþ.

4: *jarkna] *so* B, C, D; iarkna, E; rokna, A, *but* jokna *is written in the margin*   5: manheim] man heim, B   6: mǫn] men, E   af] of, E   7: dro leik] droleik, E

Mögur Dellings framkeyrði jó, settan dýrum jarknasteinum; mön mars glóar af of mannheim, drösull dró leik Dvalins í reið.

Dellingur's son (Dagur, day) drove forward his steed, adorned with precious jewels; the horse's mane shines from it across the world of men, his charger drew Dvalinn's plaything (the sun) in a chariot.

25. Jormungrund*ar*
 i *jodyr nyrdra
 und rŏt ytstu
 adalþollar
 gengo til reckio
 gygiur *ok* þursar,
 nair, dverg*ar*
 ok dockalf*ar*.

1: Jormungrund*ar*] Jormun grundar, B, C   2: *jodyr] *so* B, C; jo dyr, D; iodyr, E; jadyr, A   nyrdra] neþra, A (*in the margin*); nyrðra, B   4: adalþollar] adal þollar, B; aþal þollar, C, D   6: gygiur] gygor, C; gygur, E

Gýgjur og þursar, náir, dvergar og dökkálfar gengu til rekkju nyrðra í jöður jörmungrundar und yztu rót aðalþollar.

Trollwives and giants, corpses, dwarves and dark-elves went to bed further north on the edge of the mighty earth under the outermost root of the foremost tree (Yggdrasill).

26. Risu racknar,
 ran*n* Alfra/þull,
 nordur ad *Niflheim
 Niola sokte;
 upp nam ar Giǫll
 Ulfrunar niþur
 hornþyt valld*ur*
 Himin biarga.

3: Niflheim] *so* B, E; Nifheim, A, *but adds* Niflheim *in the margin*; Niblheim, C ad *Niflheim] Niflheim i, D   5: upp nam] upprann, E   ar Giǫll] argiǫll, A, B, C, D; argioll, E   6: Ulfrunar] ulfrimar, B   8: Himin] Himni, B, C

Raknar risu, Alfröðull rann, Njóla sótti norður að Niflheim; ár nam upp niður Úlfrúnar, valdur Himinbjarga, hornþyt Gjöll.

The gods rose up, Álfröðull (the sun) rose, Njóla (darkness, i.e. night) went north to Niflheimur; early Úlfrún's son (Heimdallur), ruler of Himinbjörg, began the sound of the horn with Gjöll (Gjallarhorn).

COMMENTARY

1. The stanza gives a picture of various beings in the world, and by way of introduction to the story we get to know that All-father (Alfǫðr is one of Óðinn's names in *Grímnismál* 48 and *SnE* I 8, but here is perhaps to be understood as the Christian God) is the one behind the plan we hear more about in st. 2. This first stanza tells us what the attitude of various beings to the plan is. That the stanza has previously been taken as an overview of the state of mind in various places in the world is implied by a paragraph that was printed under the heading 'Frjettir' ('News') in the weekly Þjóðólfur, 16. November 1849, 108. The report, obviously modelled on st. 1 of *Hrafnagaldur*, is supposed to characterise some of the most important cities in the northern hemisphere.

Kaupmannahöfn spýtir mórauðu. Kristjania æpir á Óðin. Stokkhólmur dregur seyminn. Pjetursborg lítur hornauga. London miðlar málum. Edinborg dreymir. Dublin betlar. Paris er í skollaleik. Amsterdam reiknar. Bryssel glottir. Madrid reykir. Lissabon akar sjer. Berlin bruggar. Vinarborg gnýstir tönnum. Varschau stynur. Rómaborg bænir sig. Konstantinopel glápir á mánann. Athenuborg áttar sig. En hvað gjörir Reykjavík? hún sjálfsagt þenkir og ályktar.

Copenhagen spits tobacco juice. Christiania yells at Óðinn. Stockholm drags it out. Petersburg looks askance. London mediates. Edinburgh dreams. Dublin begs. Paris is playing blind man's buff. Amsterdam is doing its sums. Brussels is smiling. Madrid is smoking. Lisbon shakes itself. Berlin is brewing. Vienna gnashes it teeth. Warsaw groans. Rome says its prayers. Constantinople gazes at the moon. Athens takes its bearings. And what is Reykjavik doing? Of course she ponders and concludes.

Þjóðólfur was founded by Sveinbjörn Hallgrímsson, who was also its editor from 1848 to 1852. He was Sveinbjörn Egilsson's nephew; he matriculated from Bessastaðir in 1834, and then lived for five years with Sveinbjörn Egilsson at Eyvindarstaðir, where he taught during the winters. Sveinbjörn Hallgrímsson had a son who was known as Hallgrímur Scheving (born 1846), though this was not the Hallgrímur Scheving (1781–1861) that edited *Hrafnagaldur*. But the boy's mother, Sveinbjörn Hallgrímsson's second wife, was daughter of Þórunn, daughter of Stefán Scheving. Possibly it was Hallgrímur Scheving, editor of *Hrafnagaldur*, that sent the anonymous news item to Þjóðólfur.

1.5: Íviðja is a name for a trollwife. It appears in a *þula* ('Trǫllkvenna heiti') in *Skáldskaparmál* (*SnE* II 112, v. 425) and in *Hyndlyljóð* 48. It may mean 'she who lives in the wood'. In *Vǫluspá* 2 we find *íviðir* (with the variant *íviðjur* in the Hauksbók version), which perhaps means 'inner timbers', referring to the roots of Yggdrasill, the World Ash.

2. The stanza should be read in conjunction with st. 1. It is All-father's plan that the Æsir discover and want to bring to nothing.

2.3: 'Verpir/verper' is the only form the manuscripts offer. It is presumably an adjective meaning 'that opposes', 'reluctant' or perhaps 'changeable', cf. *verpa* 'to throw', *litverpur* 'changeable in colour'. It must refer to the gods.

2.5: Óðhrærir ('mind-mover') appears in *Hávamál* 107 and 140 in the form Óðrerir, where it means first an intoxicating drink (the mead of poetry) which Óðinn drinks after his ritual hanging, and then the drink's container. According to *Skáldskaparmál* (*SnE* II 3/21 and 14/11), Oðreyrir was one of the vessels in which the dwarves saved Kvasir's blood, while in *SnE* II 4/3 it is again one of the vessels containing the mead of poetry. In *Hrafnagaldur* 2, Óðhrærir is apparently taken to be a person, probably a dwarf in the world of the gods, since we are told that he has to look after Urður, unless it is a case of a double scribal error for 'Oðhræres skylde Urd*u*r gejma' which would require two emendations. It is more likely that the poet misunderstood, or deliberately changed, the role of Óðhrærir. He may be supposed to be be a figure of deception, somebody who can change the appearance of things.

2.6: Urðr is known as one of the three maidens, Urðr, Verðandi, Skuld (*Vǫluspá* 20), often identified as the Norns in charge of fate, Past (cf. *urðu*, past plural of *verða*), Present and Future. See also *Gylfaginning* ch. 15, *SnE* I 18/13. In *Vǫluspá* 19 Urðar brunnr ('Urðr's spring or well') lies under the ash Yggdrasill (cf. *Gylfaginning* chs 15 and 16, *SnE* I 17/30, 19/27 and 29). In *Loddfáfnismál*, *Hávamál* 111, the speaker has to chant while sitting on the 'þulr's' ('wise man's) seat at Urðar brunnr.

2.7: 'máttkat' is the 1st pers. sg. of the past tense of the verb *mega* 'be able', with the suffixed pronoun -*k* (for *ek*) and suffixed negative -*at* = *mátta-ek-at* 'I could not' (the form is slightly anomalous; it would normally have been *máttigat*). The suffixed negative -*a*, -*at* or -*t*, like the suffixed 1st pers. sg. pron. -*k*, was obsolete by the seventeenth century, and here must be a deliberate archaism by the poet, who has through his ignorance used the 1st pers. form instead of the 3rd pers., which would have been *máttit*.

3. As a continuation from the preceding stanza, we are told how Óðhrærir's courage fails as a result of his inability to control fate, and that he therefore looks for the other dwarves. The second half of the stanza is apparently about two of these dwarves and their feelings, which are probably portents of what is going to happen. This reading is supported by the fact that st. 4 actually opens with the end of the dwarves.

3.5: All manuscripts except B have 'Þranis', but this is an unknown name. 'Þráinn' is a dwarf name, known from *Vǫluspá* 12 (in *Gylfaginning* ch. 14, *SnE* I 16/23 we find the name Þorinn instead, but Þróinn appears a little later in the same *þula*, 16/26). Besides, Þráinn rhymes with the next name, 'Dáinn', which supports the assumption that this form is correct. 'Þránis' probably arose from the misreading of the minims. In Helgi Ólafsson's Latin translation in 34 Þráinn is rendered Odinus.

3.7: Dáinn is a dwarf name that is found in the Hauksbók and *Gylfaginning* (ch. 14, *SnE* I 16/17) versions of the same *þula* in *Vǫluspá* as Þráinn is found in. It is also found in *Hyndluljóð* 7. A Dáinn carves runes for the elves in *Hávamál* 143. In *Grímnismál* 33 it is the name of a stag, and finally it is found as a fox name in a *þula*. It means 'dead'.

4. The dwarves disappear from the story, and attention is turned to the worlds (nine according to *Gylfaginning* chs 3, 34, *SnE* I 9/5, 27/15; *Vǫluspá* 2; *Vafþrúðnismál* 43), which are swallowed up into the abyss.

Commentary

4.1: The statement that there is no more to be said of the dwarves reminds one of the conclusion of one of the *þulur* in *Vǫluspá* 12: 'Nú hefi ek dverga . . . rétt um talða' ('Now I have correctly enumerated the dwarves'), and again in *Vǫluspá* 30: 'Nú eru talðar nǫnnur Herjans' ('Now have been listed Herjan's (Óðinn's) maidens (the valkyries)').

4.3: *Ginnungr* or *ginnungi* in 'Ginnungagap' (*Vǫluspá* 3; *Gylfaginning* chs 5, 8, 15, *SnE* I 10/12, 11/36, 17/13) and 'Ginnungahiminn' (*Gylfaginning* ch. 8, *SnE* I 12/8), probably meant originally 'of the mighty space(s)' or 'filled with illusion or magical power' (cf. *ginning*; see *SnE* I 100; *LP* 182), which is probably how the poet intended it to be taken here. Later the word was sometimes understood to be the name of a person. In *rímur*, Ginnungur was used as a name for Óðinn (see Finnur Jónsson 1926–28, 132). In *þulur* it turns up as a hawk name.

4.5: Alsviðr is the name of one of the horses of the sun (*Grímnismál* 37; *Gylfaginning* ch. 11, *SnE* I 14/1). This does not fit the context here, but *alsviðr* could mean 'all-wise', which would be a plausible name for Óðinn, though it is not recorded as such elsewhere, and the activity in this stanza would fit well with one of his characteristic roles in mythology: he decides who shall die, and he gathers the fallen to himself in Valhǫll. If it is Óðinn that is meant here, it would appear that the poet imagined the gods to dwell in the sky ('ofan' in line 6).

5. St. 5 gives a vision of the end of the world, which seems now imminent. Several elements in the stanza, among others the idea that knowledge is hidden in Mímir's spring, are reminiscent of *Vǫluspá*. The syntax is involved, so that the style is like that of a skaldic poem.

5.2. 'Strind' is a poetic word for land, 'rǫðull' is one for the sun (*SnE* II 37/25, 85/19, 133/30).

5.3. Cf. *Vǫluspá* 25: 'lopt allt lævi blandit'.

5.5–6. Cf. *Vǫluspá* 28 (Codex Regius), quoted in *Gylfaginning*, *SnE* I 17. 'Mærr brunnr Mímis' is where Óðinn has hidden his eye, and that stanza actually ends with the prophetess's words 'Vituð ér enn eða hvat?', which come almost word for word in line 8 here. We are told in the same stanza of *Vǫluspá* that Mímir drinks mead every morning from Valfǫðr's (Óðinn's) pledge, but it is not there, but in Snorri's accompanying prose (*SnE* I 17/16–18), that we are told that wisdom and human intelligence are hidden in Mímir's spring, and that Mímir drinks from it using the horn Gjallarhorn. In another account of Mímir, in *Ynglinga saga* (*Heimskringla* I 12–13, 18), Snorri says he was decapitated by the Vanir, after which Óðinn embalmed his head, and then used it afterwards as a sort of adviser (cf. also Mímir's head in *Vǫluspá* 46 and *Sigrdrífumál* 14).

5.7. The wise being is perhaps Iðunn, introduced more specifically in the next stanza. But Helgi Ólafsson in 34 gives as an alternative translation of 'vissa vera', 'certa essentia' ('certain existence'). According to *Orðabók Háskólans*, the adjectives *vís* and *viss* in various of their meanings in the sixteenth and seventeenth centuries were interchangeable (for instance 'dauðinn er vís', in Marteinn Einarsson's *Ein Kristilig handbog*, København 1555; 'Gvd hann er einungis | eilijf Guddomleg vera | almaattug | vijs | sannarleg', in *Enchiridion*, translated by Guðbrandur Þorláksson and printed in 1600 at Hólar). So the meaning of 'vissa vera' here could possibly be 'the wise being', 'certain existence' or perhaps 'secure existence'. The idea is maybe that secure existence is hidden in Mímir's spring, or in other words humanity's knowledge of the future life is concealed.

6. Stt. 2–4 described the ominous events taking place in the world as a prelude to the action of the poem. With st. 6, Iðunn, one of the chief figures in the story, is introduced. We are told that she has come down from the ash Yggdrasill.

6.3: Yggdrasill is the well known ash-tree of Norse mythology, which according to *Vǫluspá* 19 stands always green above Urðr's spring. According to *Grímnismál* 31 it has three roots, under one of which is Hel, under the second the frost giants, under the third human beings. Snorri says it is the biggest of trees (cf. *Grímnismál* 44), and he adds that its branches spread out over all the world and across the sky. According to him, of its three roots one is among the Æsir, the second among the frost giants and the third extends across Niflheimr; Mímir's spring is under the second (*Gylfaginning* ch. 15, *SnE* I 17).

6.6: Iðunn appears in only one of the eddic poems besides *Hrafnagaldur*, and that one is *Lokasenna*, according to the prose introduction to which she is the wife of the god Bragi (so also *Gylfaginning* ch. 26, *SnE* I 25). In *Lokasenna* 17 Loki accuses her of having made love to her brother's slayer. She is best known from the story in *Skáldskaparmál*, *SnE* II 1–2 (alluded to in *Haustlǫng*, *SnE* II 32–33), of how Loki lured her out of Ásgarðr into a forest from where the giant Þjazi was able to carry off both her and her magical apples that had the power to keep the gods forever young.

6.7: The name Ívaldr is known from *Grímnismál* 43 and Snorri's *Edda* in the form Ívaldi. Though his nature is never explicitly stated (cf. Finnur Jónsson in *LP*: 'ukendt mytisk person'), Snorri says (*SnE* I 36/16–17, II 41/33–34; both passages based on *Grímnismál* 43, which he quotes in *SnE* II 18–19) that his sons are dwarves; they were the makers of the ship Skíðblaðnir.

7. The stanza tells us that Iðunn did not care for her sojourn under Yggdrasill, where she is imprisoned at Night's home (i.e. held in darkness).

7.6: *Kundr*, according to Snorri (*SnE* II 107/18) is a word for 'relative'. Cf. *LP*.

Nǫrvi (or Nǫrfi/Narfi) is known from *Gylfaginning* ch. 10 (*SnE* I 13/22–23) as a giant who lived in Jǫtunheimar and was father of Nótt (Night); the corresponding figure in *Vafþrúðnismál* 25 and *Alvíssmál* 29 is Nǫrvi in the dative, which would be Nǫrr in the nominative. Nótt, who is black and dark, was first of all married to Naglfari, then to Annarr/Ánarr/Ónarr (their son was Jǫrð, Earth), and finally to Dellingr (their son was Dagr, Day). 'Nǫrvi's son' is a kenning for night.

8.1: 'Sigtívar' is the plural of *sigtýr*, 'battle- or victory-god' (*Vǫluspá* 44; the singular is also a name for Óðinn). In *Grímnismál* 45 and *Lokasenna* 1 the gods are referred to as 'sigtíva synir'.

8.2: The singular Nanna is the name of Baldr's wife, and she is listed among goddesses in *Skáldskaparmál* (*SnE* II 114, v. 434). Snorri says that she and Baldr were parents of Forseti (*Gylfaginning* ch. 32, *SnE* I 26/24); Nanna died of grief at Baldr's funeral (*Gylfaginning* ch. 49, *SnE* I 46/33). She is nevertheless present (though Baldr and Hǫðr are not) at the feast for Ægir at the beginning of *Skáldskaparmál*. Nanna also appears in Saxo's version of the story of Balderus and Høtherus in *Gesta Danorum* III 1–4; she was beloved by Balderus but married to Høtherus. A Nanna (MS *manna*) Nǫkkvadóttir is mentioned in *Hyndluljóð* 20. In *Vǫluspá* 30 *nanna* is used in the plural ('nǫnnur Herjans' 'Óðinn's ladies') of valkyries. Finally, in *rímur* and skaldic kennings *nanna* means 'woman', and that is probably what it means here. It presumably refers to Iðunn.

8.3: 'Viggjar' (genitive of *vigg* 'horse') must refer to Yggdrasill, from which Iðunn came down. *Yggdrasill* is thought to mean 'Yggr's (Óðinn's) horse', the steed Óðinn was 'riding' when he was hanging on the tree. We were told in st. 7 that Iðunn was under the tree.

8.4: According to Hallgrímur Scheving (1837, 13), the poet is trying to depict the gods in a ridiculous light by their treating Iðunn as a witch ('galdranorn') in among other things sending her a wolf skin, but also by showing them chanting spells and riding on wolves (st. 10).

9. The stanza says that Óðinn chose Heimdallur to ask the woman what she knew about the world, while Bragi and Loki are filled with apprehension.

9.1: Viðrir is a name for Óðinn (*Lokasenna* 26; *Gylfaginning* ch. 3, *SnE* I 8/32; *Ágrip* 3/14; *Flateyjarbók* I 564/15).

9.2: Bifrǫst is the name of the gods' bridge from the earth to heaven, which Snorri equates with a rainbow (*Gylfaginning* ch. 13, *SnE* I 15/4–15), adding (*Gylfaginning* ch. 27, *SnE* I 25/36–37) that Heimdallr is the gods' guardian at the bridge against the giants. In eddic poems (*Grímnismál* 44, *Fáfnismál* 15) the bridge is called Bilrǫst, and it is not specially associated with Heimdallr. The name of the bridge does not appear in any skaldic kennings for Heimdallr either (Meissner 1921, 255).

9.3–4: *Gjǫll* (genitive *gjallar*) is found as the first element in the name of Heimdallr's horn, Gjallarhorn, and also as the name of a river that must be crossed on the road to Hel (*Grímnismál* 28; *Gylfaginning* ch. 49, *SnE* I 47/8–10). It is the latter meaning that is relevant here. The sun of a river is a kenning for gold (*Skáldskaparmál* ch. 33 and verse 391/2, *SnE* II 41 and 101), and gold's support (or doorpost; a variation of the commoner 'tree of gold', which refers to the fashion of women wearing gold ornaments) is a kenning for a woman. *Gátt* is often used in *rímur* in kennings for women (see Finnur Jónsson 1926–1928, 125).

9.7: The poet Bragi is according to *Grímnismál* 44 the most outstanding of poets, but the god Bragi only appears in the eddic poems in *Lokasenna*. In Snorri's *Edda* he is the god most knowledgeable about poetry, and Iðunn is his wife. Loptr is another name for Loki.

10. We are told that the gods set out, though Óðinn evidently stays behind. We are also told that the gods chanted spells ('regin gólu galdur'). It is perhaps conceivable that the title of the poem was originally 'Ragnagaldur' rather than 'Hrafnagaldur'.

10.2: 'gandr' has sometimes been taken to mean 'wolf', but here is more likely to mean something analogous to a witch's broomstick. Cf. *gandreið* in *Njáls saga* ch. 125 and the poem *Gandreið* by Jón Daðason (1606–1676).

10.3: Rǫgnir is a name for Óðinn, found in skaldic verse and *þulur* (*SnE* 1848–1887, II 472, 556). Regin (n. pl.) means gods (see *Gylfaginning* ch. 8, *SnE* I 12, where Snorri quotes *Grímnismál* 40–41 on the creation of the world). Reginn (m. sg.) is the name of a dwarf (*Vǫluspá* 12), Fáfnir's brother (*SnE* II 45–47; *Reginsmál* prose introduction; cf. *SnE* 1848–1887, II 470, 553). In *Hrafnagaldur* 10.3, 'regin' must be the correct form. In late manuscripts 'n' is commonly written with a nasal stroke.

10.4: The preposition *at* in the meaning 'towards' or 'up to' takes the dative, but here 'rann' is anomalously accusative (cf. the variant in E), though it might be dative of the Modern Icelandic *rannur* (strong masc. nouns often lack the ending *-i*). Finnur Jónsson 1926–1928 quotes *rann himins* as meaning 'himmerige' ('heaven'). 'Rann(ur) heimis' (literally the mansion of the world; *heimi* is a variant form of *heimr*; see Ásgeir Blöndal Magnússon 1989) in this stanza can be understood as 'dwelling place of the world', i.e. the earth, if the gods are here descending to the earth from heaven (cf. *SnE* I 15/5). Alternatively, it may be just a variant of *rann himins*, referring to the sky as the roof over the world; the gods would then be flying across the sky on their magic poles. Cf. *glyggrann* ('the house of the wind', 'the sky'), *SnE* II 77/8.

10.6: Hliðskjálf is Óðinn's lookout place in Válaskjálf, whence he can see over all the world(s) (cf. the prose introductions to *Grímnismál* and *Skírnismál*; *SnE* I 13, 20, 31, 48). The name is also found in skaldic kennings for Óðinn (*SnE* II 11), but not in medieval eddic verse.

11.1: The objects of *frá* are *banda burða* and *brauta sinna*.

11.2: *selja* is a common base word in kennings for woman, but it is uncertain whether originally it meant the tree (willow) or the verbal noun 'giver, server'. Serving of drink was one of the conventional roles of women in the Viking Age and later. See *Skáldskaparmál* ch. 31, especially *SnE* II 40/16–21.

11.3: *Bǫnd* (n. pl.) 'gods'. *Burðir* (m. pl.; related to the verb *bera* 'bear') can mean either 'birth, extraction' or 'offspring'.

11.5: Hlýrnir was the sixth of the nine mythological heavens (see *SnE* II 133). Hel was the abode of the dead, and also the name of the daughter of Loki who presided over the world of the dead.

11.7: *Ártíð* 'death day' was the word in Christian times for the anniversary of a person's death, which in the case of saints was often made a feast day (*ONP* I 584–585); together with st. 14.8 'sókn', it is evidence that the poem does not belong to the thought world of heathendom.

12. The stanza tells us that Iðunn does not speak a word, so that the gods get no answer to their questions. Instead she begins to weep.

12.1–4: The unstressed proclitic negative adverb *ne* would have had a short vowel in Old Icelandic (see Ásgeir Blöndal Magnússon 1989).

12.3: Rask suggested that 'givom' should be emended to 'tívom' (dat. pl. of *týr* 'god'). The adjective *gifr* 'greedy' is only deduced from a doubtful reading in *Fjölsvinnsmál* 13, and occurs nowhere else. It is supported by the adjective *gifre* 'greedy' in Old English, and would fit the context here well (= greedy for answers, referring to the gods), but the '-r' is radical, and the dat. would be *gífrum*. Perhaps the author mistook the inflection class in his reading of *Fjölsvinnsmál*.

Commentary

12.6: *Targa* (f.) 'targe', a kind of round shield; 'shields of the forehead' is a kenning for eyes (see *SnE* II 108/11–12). *Hjarn* or *hjarni* (m.) 'brain', 'skull', 'dome of the head' *SnE* II 108/10–12. *Orðabók Háskólans* has examples from folk poetry of the seventeenth century and later of 'hjarnar stjörnur' as a kenning for eyes.

12.7: Rask suggested taking 'eliun faldin' as one word ('with her energy hidden'?), but reading 'endurrjóða eljunfeldinn' ([they, i.e. the tears] make the energy-cloak red again' is also perhaps possible, taking *eljunfeldur* 'cloak of energy' as a kenning for eyelid or cheek (cf. *eljunstrǫnd* 'beach (i.e. seat) of energy', = breast *LP* and Finnur Jónsson 1926–28, 76). *Eljun* appears in *SnE* II 108/31 as a *heiti* for *hugr*, so perhaps 'eljunfeldur' means 'cloak of the mind' = eye or eyelid.

13. In stt. 13 and 14 Iðunn's silence and weeping are compared with the magical thorn that every night causes all the world to sleep, here brought by the dwarf Dáinn. This myth is not found elsewhere, but cf. the folk-tale *svefnþorn* ('sleep thorn') that causes deep sleep, like the spindle in Sleeping Beauty.

13.1: The stanza opens an epic simile that continues into the next stanza ('Eins . . .', 'Likewise . . .'). Scheving suggested adding 'ok' after 'Eins' ('Just as . . .')

13.2: Élivágar are primeval waters (rivers, according to Snorri) associated with creation myths (*Gylfaginning* ch. 5, *SnE* I 9–10; *Vafþrúðnismál* 31; *SnE* II 22/25; cf. *Hymiskviða* 5).

13.3: Þorn is the name of a giant in *Þórsdrápa* (*SnE* II 27–28) and elsewhere. A *svefnþorn* is found in several Old Norse sources, for example Gǫngu-Hrólfr is pricked to sleep with one (*Gǫngu-Hrólfs saga* ch. 24), and in *Vǫlsunga saga* ch. 21, Brynhildr says that Óðinn had pricked her with such a thorn. Scheving suggested (1837, 43) interpreting 'þorn' in this stanza as a *svefnþorn*, and that the hrime-cold giant might be Njǫrvi, Night's father. In view of the medieval Icelandic concept of the *svefnþorn* and this stanza's mention of 'every night' when the thorn is used, it seems likely that 'þorn' is to be regarded as a metaphor for sleep. The emendation of 'atri' to 'acri' was suggested by Scheving too ('c' and 't' are almost identical in gothic script). It might also be possible to emend to 'hatri'.

13.6: Dáinn: see commentary on st. 3/7.

13.7: Miðgarðr is the rampart made by the gods out of the primeval giant's eyelashes surrounding the world of men and protecting it from giants (*Gylfaginning* ch. 8, *SnE* I 12; *Grímnismál* 41). It may originally have meant 'Middle-earth' (Old English *middangeard*), the world of men between the worlds of gods and giants (Ásgarðr in the centre and Útgarðr round the outside). *Garðr* means 'an enclosure, an enclosed space'.

13/8: It might be possible to emend this line to 'miðnætti hvert', 'every midnight'.

14. The stanza continues the simile of st. 13. It is a description of the effects of sleep. When the people of the world are overcome by sleep, they are deprived of the power to act and insensibility floods their minds, and the whole parish is as it were rocked to sleep.

14.4: 'Hvíti Áss', the white god, is Heimdallr (*SnE* I 25/32; *Þrymskviða* 15/2). 'Heimdallr's sword' is a kenning for head (*SnE* I 26/1, II 19/11, 108/8–9). At *SnE* II 19/11 Snorri adds 'Svá er sagt at hann var lostinn manns hǫfði í gegnum' 'It is said that he was struck through with a human head', but no further explanation of this curious idea is given, any more than there is of the next kenning (line 6).

14.5: The noun *örvit* is recorded in *Orðabók Háskólans* from the seventeenth century onwards, but *ONP* has a citation of *ørvit* from c. 1350.

14.6: 'Rýgjar glyggvi' (dative) 'wind of the trollwife' is a kenning for thought (*SnE* II 108/28–30), though its origin is unknown. Both this kenning and 'Heimdallr's sword' as a kenning for head appear in the same passage in *Skáldskaparmál* (chs 69–70, *SnE* II 108) as the comparatively rare uses of 'hjarn(i) and 'eljun' (st. 12). This suggests that the poet was using Snorri's *Edda* as a textbook for poetic language while he wrote. The lack of *j* after a palatalised *g* as in 'rýgar' is found elsewhere, though rarely; but the number of occurrences makes it unlikely that they are all scribal errors; cf. p. 65 above. See Noreen 1923, §263, Anm. 2; Bandle 1956, 128 (§82.3) and 140 (§89.3).

14.8: 'sókn' f. 'parish (in the Christian Church)'. Cf. the comments on st. 11.7 above.

15. Jórunn's state is compared with the state of sleep just described: She seems to be prostrated by grief, as if she were unconscious. When the gods could not get an answer to their questions to Iðunn, they begged harder, but this did no good.

15.1: With the introductory 'Jamt' (= jafnt, 'just so') this stanza is linked to the epic simile (introduced by 'Eins' 'Likewise') in the two preceding ones.

Jormi is a name not recorded elsewhere at all, and its function here would be a complete mystery. Scheving suggested that it might be an error for Jórun, cf. the reading of E (there has been a mistake in reading the four minims which any of the scribes could have made). Rask wondered whether it could be an error for Jórunn or Iðunn (a single *n* for *nn* is not uncommon in manuscripts of this date). Since the name Jórunn does not appear elsewhere in the poem, and the context here requires a reference to Iðunn, it may be that the poet meant Jórunn to be another name (or a *heiti*) for Iðunn (cf. the alternatives Nál and Laufey); otherwise the only possible explanation is that it is a scribal error.

15.2: Jólnar (m. pl.) is a name for the gods (*SnE* II 85/3–4).

15.4: 'geta' in this sense normally takes an acc. object; cf. st. 21.8.

16. The stanza tells us that Heimdallur now leaves, taking Loki with him. Bragi on the other hand stays behind to observe the woman.

16.3, 7: Herjan and Grímnir (and Grímr) are well known names for Óðinn (*SnE* I 21–22, *Grímnismál* 46–47 and elsewhere). Grímir is not recorded as one of his names, and must be a scribal error.

16.4: Gjallarhorn is the horn that Heimdallr blows when Ragnarǫk is imminent (*SnE* I 50/22–24; *Vǫluspá* 46, quoted in *SnE* I 51). According to Snorri, Mímir drinks mead from his spring out of it (*SnE* I 17/17–18), but it is not said elsewhere that it belongs to Óðinn. When Heimdallr's nature and functions, along with those of the other gods, are described, it is said that when he blows the horn it can be heard throughout all the worlds (*SnE* I 25–26).

16.5: Nál is an alternative name for Loki's mother Laufey (*SnE* I 26/36–37, II 19/35–36; see also *Sǫrla þáttr*, *Flateyjarbók* I 275/27). It is pointed out by Bugge (*Norrœn fornkvæði* 1867, 374, note), that the author could have taken the form

Commentary

'nepa' from the Codex Regius of Snorri's *Edda*, where *nepi* is found as a spelling of *nefi* (see *SnE* 1931, 188/17 and textual note). In both places the *p* may have arisen from the misunderstanding of an insular *f*.

16.8: *Grund* (f.) 'ground' is a half-kenning for 'woman', i.e. it is frequently found as the base word in kennings for woman such as 'grund bauga', 'grund gulls', and here the base word is used without a determinant. Half-kennings are not all that uncommon; see *SnE* II 51, v. 155/6 *runna* and note.

17. We are told that Heimdallur and Loki now enter Vingólf, having been conveyed there by the winds, i.e. they have flown (cf. st. 10 above).

17.1: The name Vingólf is not found in medieval poetry, either eddic or skaldic. Snorri gives conflicting information: in *Gylfaginning* ch. 3 (*SnE* I 9/3) it is an alternative name for Gimlé, a place in heaven; in *Gylfaginning* ch. 14 (*SnE* I 15/25–26) it is a sanctuary owned by *gyðjur* (goddesses or priestesses); in *Gylfaginning* ch. 20 (*SnE* I 21/29), it is to Valhǫll and Vingólf that Óðinn sends his 'einherjar' (champions, dead heroes that will fight for the gods at Ragnarǫk).

17.2: Viðarr (or Víðarr) is a son of Óðinn (*Vǫluspá* 55; prose introduction to *Lokasenna*; *SnE* II 19/23–25). He is known as the silent god (*SnE* I 26/15); he will kill the wolf Fenrir after the latter has killed Óðinn (*SnE* I 50–52; *Vǫluspá* 55). Rask was in favour of emending 'Viþars' to 'Viþris'; Scheving proposed 'Viþurs' (Viðrir and Viðurr are both names of Óðinn). Bugge thought the poet might have arbitrarily used the name Viðarr for Óðinn.

17.3: Fornjótr was a giant (*SnE* II 111, v. 419/5), father of wind and fire and sea (*SnE* II 39/13–15). See *Orkneyinga saga* chs 1–3. 'Fornjotr's kinsmen' is a kenning for winds.

17.7: Yggr is a name of Óðinn (see for example *Grímnismál* 53, *SnE* I 22/12).

17.8: Scheving (1837, 17) thought it was remarkable that the gods sat merrily drinking in this grave situation, while in st. 21 they are so troubled about the expedition's failure. He claimed their unconcerned drinking feast was reminiscent of the behaviour of the Greco–Roman gods who, in contrast to their Nordic counterparts, did not need to worry about the future.

18. Almost the whole of the stanza is indirect speech, the greeting of the newcomers to Óðinn and the rest of the gods.

18.1: Hangatýr is a name of Óðinn (*SnE* II 5/19–23; in skaldic verse but not in medieval eddic poems).

18.3: The word for wort or mash, the mixture of powdered malt and water before fermentation into beer, in Old Icelandic is *virtr* (n., dat. sg. *virtri*, *Sigrdrífumál* 17). *Virt* (f., dat. *virt*, same meaning), used here, is recorded in *Orðabók Háskólans* in texts, mostly *rímur*, from the sixteenth century onwards. In this poem the word is used to mean the beer itself (metonymy).

18.6: *Díar* (m. pl), 'gods', appears in a list of names for gods in *SnE* II 85/8, quoting a verse of Kormakr (v. 308). Also used in *Heimskringla*, *Ynglinga saga* ch. 2).

18.7: Yggjungr is a name of Óðinn (*Vǫluspá* 28, but not mentioned in Snorri's *Edda*).

19.2: Bǫlverkr is a name of Óðinn (*Hávamál* 109; *Grímnismál* 47; *SnE* I 22/2, II 4).

19.3–4: *Grímnismál* 18 mentions that the *einherjar* feed on meat from Sæhrímnir. In *Gylfaginning* ch.38 (*SnE* I 32) this stanza is quoted, and Snorri explains that Sæhrímnir is a boar that is cooked every day and whole again every evening, so that there is always enough for the *einherjar* to eat.

19.4: Rakni is the name of a sea-king, but his crew have no place here. It must be a spelling for *ragna*, gen. of *regin* 'gods'. Cf. st. 26/1 and commentary. 'Sjót ragna' may mean the *einherjar*, to whom Óðinn assigns seats in Valhǫll (*SnE* I 21/19).

19.5: Skǫgul is a valkyrie (*Vǫluspá* 30; used in skaldic poetry in kennings for battle, weapons and armour). In *Grímnismál* 36 (quoted in *SnE* I 30) Skǫgul is mentioned among the valkyries that serve ale to the *einherjar*, and in that poem the suffering Óðinn wishes they could bring him a drink.

19.6: Hnikarr is a name of Óðinn (*Grímnismál* 47, quoted in *SnE* I 21; *SnE* I 8/30). The name is used in skaldic verse in kennings for, among other things, battle.

20.4: 'Hǫrgar' (m. pl.) means 'sanctuaries, holy places', but the context requires a word meaning 'gods' (it is difficult to see that *hǫrgar* were particularly associated with goddesses, cf. *LP*). Either the word means 'holy ones' by metonymy (deities were worshipped in holy places), or the poet was mistaken about its usage.

20.8: 'huma' is an emendation suggested by Rask.

22.1: Ómi is a name of Óðinn in various lists in verse and prose (*SnE* I 8/31; *Grímnismál* 49, quoted in *SnE* I 22; *SnE* 1848–87, II 472, 556).

22.3–4. See the discussion of this proverb on pp. 18–21.

23. The first half of the stanza at least is probably corrupt; Bugge's attempt at interpretation (*Norrœn fornkvæði* 1867, 375) involves unprecedented reordering of the words and can hardly be right: 'Fenris fóðr (i.e. sól) rann með röstum Rindar (i.e. westwards, cf. *Baldrs draumar* 11); valla (i.e. varla) kvöddu goðin Hropt ok Frigg, géngu (i.e. ok géngu) frá gildi, sem (i.e. þá er) móðir Jarðar (i.e. nótt) fór Hrímfaxa' 'The sun went to the west, and the gods hardly said goodbye to Óðinn and Frigg, before they were gone from the feast, when night departed with Hrímfaxi.'

23.1: *röst* is a measure of distance, comparable with a league; *renna með röstum* would appear to mean 'run with league-long strides'.

23.2: Rindr is mother of Óðinn's son Váli who avenges Baldr (*SnE* I 26/18, II 19/26, 114; *Baldrs draumar* 11). She appears also in Saxo's account (*Gesta Danorum* III, 1–4) of Balderus and Høtherus. Nothing is known of her mother, but like Rindr, she was probably a giantess (cf. *SnE* II 30/10 and note). Scheving suggested reading 'móþr' for 'moþir'.

23.3: *föður* is a rare form for the nominative *faðir*. 'larður' is only known in the phrase 'e–m sígur larður' 'one becomes weary'. The word here is perhaps an error for or an alternative form of the past participle *laraður* 'wearied'. *Orðabók Háskólans* has examples of both words from the seventeenth to twentieth centuries).

23.4: Fenrir, son of Loki and the giantess Angrboða (*SnE* I 27/4–5), is the wolf that kills Óðinn and destroys the sun at Ragnarǫk (*Vǫluspá* 53; *SnE* I 50; *Vafþrúðnismál* 47, quoted in *SnE* I 54), and it is he that bites off Týr's hand (*Lokasenna* 38; *SnE* I 25/14–19).

23.7: Hroptr is a name of Óðinn (in a verse from Kormakr's *Sigurðardrápa* quoted in *SnE* II 10; *Vǫluspá* 62; *Grímnismál* 8; *SnE* 1848–87, II 472, 555). Frigg is Óðinn's wife (*SnE* I 5/17–18, 13/14, 21/18 and elsewhere).

23.8: Hrímfaxi is the name of a horse that carries Night across the sky (*Vafþrúðnismál* 14; *SnE* I 13/30, II 90/1–2). 'Fór Hrímfaxa (dat.)' presumably means 'went at the same time as the night, i.e. at dawn'. Since the verb 'fór' is singular, it must refer only to Frigg, oddly enough; unless Loki is meant.

24.2: Dellingr is father of Dagr (day) (*Vafþrúðnismál* 25; *SnE* I 13/25–26).

24.5: *mannheimr* is only otherwise recorded as pl. Mannheimar, *Ynglinga saga* ch. 8, *Heimskringla* I 21/12 (here Manheimar, perhaps 'world of love', *Háleygjatal* 3), 22/6; probably taken to mean the world of men, as opposed to Goðheim(a)r (recorded both as sg. and pl.), the world of gods.

24.5–6: clearly based on *Vafþrúðnismál* 12/6 'ey lýsir mǫn af mari', which shows that 'af' means 'from the horse' (cf. *Norrœn fornkvæði* 1867, 375).

24.7: Dvalinn is the name of a dwarf (*Vǫluspá* 11, 14, the first quoted in *SnE* I 16; *Hávamál* 143), and also of a hart (*SnE* I 18/34–35). In *Fáfnismál* 13 (quoted in *SnE* I 18), some of the norns were daughters of Dvalinn. In *Alvíssmál* 16 and *SnE* II 133, v. 517/8, 'Dvalinn's leika' is a kenning for the sun. *Leika* in these sources may be the n. noun *leika* 'plaything, toy', or, in *SnE*, f. *leika* 'female playmate'; in *Alvíssmál* the word is accusative and could be from a m. noun *leiki* 'deluder' (the sun turns dwarves to stone at sunrise; see *Glossary to the Poetic Edda* 1992, 158). The endingless form *leik* in *Hrafnagaldur* may be an error, or it could be acc. of *leikr* 'game, play' meaning by metonymy 'the one/thing played with' (cf. *Norrœn fornkvæði* 1867, 375).

24.8: *drǫsull* or *drasill* m. 'horse' is used as the name of a horse ridden by 'Dagi' (presumably a variant of 'Dagr') in a *þula* ascribed to a poem called *Alsvinnsmál* in *SnE* II 89 (although Snorri also refers to *Alvíssmál* as *Alsvinnsmál*, the two poems are quite distinct).

25. The mentioning of the different beings is reminiscent of st. 1, indicating that a closure of the poem is approaching.

25.1: Jǫrmungrund 'the mighty earth'. The word is used in among other places *Grímnismál* 20, quoted in *SnE* I 32.

25.2: 'jodyr' must be derived from *Vǫluspá* 5/4 'iodýr', where it is probably intended as *jǫður* (acc.) 'edge' (the 'y' could have been copied from a variant form of 'u'; cf. *Norrœn fornkvæði* 1867, 375). This was read as 'iódýr' in *Edda* 1787–1828. In neither place can the word have anything to do with horses or doors.

25.4: Aðalþollr: cf. *Grímnismál* 44: 'Askr Yggdrasils, hann er œztr viða' 'The ash Yggdrasill, it is the highest (i.e. noblest) of trees'.

25.6: 'Gýgjur' is anomalous; the pl. of *gýgr* is *gýgjar* or *gýgir*.

25.8: cf. *SnE* I 19/38: 'døkkálfar eru svartari en bik', 'dark-elves are blacker than pitch'. They are only known from Snorri's *Edda* and *Hrafnagaldur*; cf. Svartálfaheimr 'world of the black-elves', *SnE* I 28/3–4. Both these kinds of elves (if they were different) were probably invented as counterparts to the *ljósálfar* 'light-elves' (like *svartálfar*, only known from Snorri's *Edda*), and were perhaps understood to be the same as dwarves (some of whom, at least, lived in Svartálfaheimr (see *SnE* I 28/3–4).

26. The final stanza tells how the day dawns and the gods get up. In the second half of the stanza, Heimdallur blows his horn early; this signals the approach of Ragnarǫk, and awakes the gods and summons them together to a council (*SnE* I 50/22–24; cf. Scheving 1837, 18). Evidently the gods have not succeeded in formulating a plan during the night.

26.1: 'racknar' must be for 'ragnar', cf. st. 19/4 'rakna' for 'ragna'. It may be that the poet took *rǫgn* (n. pl.) as f. nom. sg. (or *regin* as *reginn*, m. nom. sg.) of the word for 'god'; both would have nom. pl. *ragnar*, rather than the usual n. pl. 'regin' or 'rǫgn'.

26.2: Álfrǫðul(l) is a name (f.) or a word (m.) for the sun, perhaps meaning 'elf-wheel' (*Vafþrúðnismál* 47, quoted in *SnE* I 54; *Skírnismál* 4; *SnE* II 85/20, 133, v. 517/7). 'Álfröðull rann' presumably means that the sun rose.

26.3: Niflheimr (world of mist or darkness) appears in *SnE* I 9/21, 10/10–11, 17/14, 27/14, but nowhere in poetry besides *Hrafnagaldur*. It is evidently a cold place (*SnE* I 10) and lies under one of the roots of Yggdrasill; Hel (cf. st. 11) was exiled there (*SnE* I 27). It was perhaps originally the same as Niflhel, a place evil ones were sent to, analogous to the Christian Hell (*SnE* I 9/4, 35/32; *Vafþrúðnismál* 43; *Baldrs draumar* 2).

26.4: In *Alvíssmál* 30, 'njól' is said to be a name for night among the gods; the stanza is quoted in *SnE* II 99, but there the name is given as 'njóla'. Both words apparently mean literally 'darkness'.

26.5: A has 'argiǫll' as one word (and similarly the other manuscripts), but this is unknown either as a common noun or name. As two words (as suggested by Bugge) it could be ár Gjǫll, 'river Gjǫll' (cf. note to 9/3–4 above), but it must surely be something to do with Heimdallr's horn Gjallarhorn here. It is probably dat. sg. of *gjöll* f. 'a kind of trumpet' (Blöndal, *Orðabók Háskólans*); perhaps a name for Heimdallr's horn (Gjallarhorn = the horn Gjǫll, cf. Askr Yggdrasils = the ash Yggdrasill). On Gjallarhorn, see note to st. 16/4 above.

26.6: Úlfrún is one of Heimdallr's mothers (*Hyndluljóð* 37; cf. *SnE* I 26/9–10).

26.8: Himinbjǫrg ('defence of or that which saves heaven') is a place at the edge of heaven next to one end of Bifrǫst (the bridge from heaven to earth). There Heimdallr is in charge and guards heaven from the approach of giants (*SnE* I 20/2–3, 25/32–37, 26/2–7 = *Grímnismál* 13).

BIBLIOGRAPHICAL REFERENCES

Aðalheiður Guðmundsdóttir (ed.). 2001. *Úlfhams saga*. Rit 53. Reykjavík: Stofnun Árna Magnússonar á Íslandi.

Ágrip af Nóregskonunga sǫgum. Ed. Bjarni Einarson. In *ÍF* XXIX 1–54.

Ásgeir Blöndal Magnússon. 1989. *Íslensk Orðsifjabók*. Reykjavík: Orðabók Háskólans.

Bandle, Oskar. 1956. *Die Sprache der Guðbrandsbiblía*. Bibliotheca Arnamagnæana XVII. Hafniæ: Ejnar Munksgaard.

Bjarni Einarsson (ed.). 1955. *Munnmælasögur 17. aldar*. Reykjavík: Fræðafélagið.

Bjarni Vilhjálmsson and Óskar Halldórsson. 1979. *Íslenskir málshættir*. Second edition. Reykjavík: Almenna bókafélagið.

Blöndal, Sigfús. 1920–1924. *Íslensk-dönsk orðabók / Islandsk-dansk ordbog*. Reykjavík: Þórarin B. Þorláksson.

'Bréf Árna Magnússonar til Íslands 1729 og fleiri skjöl hans í Ríkisskjalasafni Dana'. 1975. Ed. Jón Margeirsson. *Opuscula* 5 (*Bibliotheca Arnamagnæana* 31), 123–180. Hafniæ: Munksgaard.

British Library. 1977. *Catalogue of Additions to the Manuscripts 1756–1782. Additional Manuscripts 4101–5017*. London: British Museum.

Den ældre Edda: En Samling af de nordiske Folks ældste Sagn og Sange, ved Sæmund Sigfussön kaldet hin Frode I–IV. 1821–1823. Trans. Finnur Magnússon. København: Gyldendal.

Den ældre Edda: Samling af norrøne Oldkvad, indeholdende Nordens ældste Gude- og Helte-Sagn. 1847. Ed. P. A. Munch. Christiania: P. T. Malling.

Die Edda: Eine Sammlung altnordischer Götter- und Heldenlieder. 1859. Ed. Hermann Lüning. Zürich: Meyer & Zeller.

Die Lieder der Edda. 1888–1906. Ed. Barend Sijmons. Halle: Verlag der Buchhandlung des Waisenhauses.

Edda Sæmundar hinns fróda I–III. 1787–1828. Ed. Guðmundur Magnæus, Jón Johnsonius, Jón Ólafsson, Finnur Magnússon & Gunnar Pálsson. Havniæ: Sumtibus Legati Arna-Magnæani et Gyldendalii.

Edda Sæmundar hinns fróda. 1818. Ed. Rasmus Kr. Rask. Holmiæ.

Edda Sæmundar hins fróða. 1860. Ed. Theodor Möbius. Leipzig: Hinrichs.

Einar G. Pétursson. 1998. *Eddurit Jóns Guðmundssonar lærða: 'Samantektir um skilning á Eddu' og 'Að fornu í þeirri gömlu norrænu kölluðust rúnir bæði ristingar og skrifelsi'. Þættir úr fræðasögu 17. aldar*. I: *Inngangur*. Rit 46. Reykjavík: Stofnun Árna Magnússonar á Íslandi.

Einar G. Pétursson. 2007. 'Akrabók: Handrit að Eddum með hendi Árna Böðvarssonar á Ökrum og hugleiðingar um handritarannsóknir á Eddunum'. *Gripla* XVIII 133–152.

Erasmus of Rotterdam. 1599. *Adagiorvm chiliades ivxta locos commvnes digestæ*. Frankfurt: Sumptibus haeredum Andreae Wecheli, Claudij Marnij, & Io. Aubrij.

Eysteinn Björnsson and William P. Reaves (eds). 2006. 'Hrafnagaldur Óðins / Forspjallsljóð': http://notendur.hi.is/eybjorn/ugm/hrg/hrg.html

Faulkes, Anthony (ed.). 1977. *Edda Islandorum. Völuspá. Hávamál.* Rit 14. Reykjavík: Stofnun Árna Magnússonar á Íslandi.

Faulkes, Anthony (ed.). 1979. *Edda Magnúsar Ólafssonar (Laufás Edda).* Rit 13. Reykjavík: Stofnun Árna Magnússonar á Íslandi.

Fidjestøl, Bjarne. 1999. *The Dating of Eddic Poetry.* Bibliotheca Arnamagnæana 41. København: C. A. Reitzels forlag.

Finnur Jónsson. 1926–1928. *Ordbog til de af Samfund til Udg. af gml. nord. Litteratur udgivne Rímur.* Samfund til Udgivelse af gammel nordisk Litteratur 51. København: Carlsbergfondet.

Finnur Jónsson. 1930. *Ævisaga Árna Magnússonar.* Safn Fræðafjelagsins VIII. København: Hið íslenska fræðafélag.

Finsen, Eyvind. 1944. *Bidrag til slægten Finsens historie med særligt henblik paa dens tilknytning til Arne Magnusson og Den arnamagnæanske Kommission. Samling af biografier, haandskrifter, slægtstavler, bogfortegnelser, litteraturfortegnelser m.m.* København: Munksgaard.

Flateyjarbók I–III. 1860–1868. Ed. Guðbrandur Vigfússon and C. R. Unger. Christiania: Malling.

Fritzner, Johan. 1883–1896. *Ordbog over det gamle norske sprog* I–III. Kristiania: Norske forlagsforening.

Glossary to the Poetic Edda. 1992. Compiled by Beatrice la Farge and John Tucker. Heidelberg: Winter.

Grímur M. Helgason (ed.). 1961. *Pontus rímur eftir Magnús Jónsson prúða, Pétur Einarsson og Síra Ólaf Halldórsson.* Reykjavík: Rímnafélagið.

Grundtvig, N. F. S. 1808. *Nordens Mytologi.* København: Schubothe.

Guðbrandur Vigfússon and Frederick York Powell. 1883. *Corpus Poeticum Boreale* I–II. Oxford: Clarendon Press.

Gödel, Vilhelm. 1892. *Katalog öfver Upsala universitets biblioteks fornisländska och fornnorska handskrifter.* Upsala: Almqvist & Wiksell.

Gödel, Vilhelm. 1897. *Fornnorsk-isländsk litteratur i Sverige* I. (*Till Antikvitetskollegiets inrättande*). Stockholm: Hæggströms boktryckeri.

Gödel, Vilhelm. 1897–1900. *Katalog öfver Kongl. Bibliotekets fornisländska och fornnorska handskrifter.* Stockholm: Kungliga biblioteket.

Hallgrímur Scheving: see Scheving, Hallgrímur.

Haukur Þorgeirsson. 2008. *Gunnarsslagur og Valagaldur Kráku: Eddukvæði frá 18. öld*. Ritgerð til BA-prófs. Íslensku og menningardeild. Hugvísindadeild Háskóla Íslands. Reykjavík. [Unpublished]

Heimskringla I–III. In *ÍF* XXVI–XXVIII.

Hughes, Shaun F. D. 1977. *Skrá um íslensk handrit í Harvard*. [Unpublished]

ÍF = Íslenzk fornrit I – . 1933– . Reykjavík: Hið íslenzka fornritafélag.

Íslendinga sögur I–II. 1843–1847. Kjøbenhavn: Det Kongelige Nordiske Oldskrift-Selskab.

Íslenzkar þjóðsögur og ævintýri I–VI. 1954–1961. Ed. Jón Árnason. New edition ed. Árni Böðvarsson and Bjarni Vilhjálmsson. Hólar: Þjóðsaga.

Íslenzkar Æviskrár I–V. 1948–1952. Compiled by Páll Eggert Ólason. Reykjavík: Hið íslenska bókmenntafélag.

Jensen, Helle (ed.). 1983. *Eiriks saga viðfǫrla*. Editiones Arnamagnæanæ B 29. København: C. A. Reitzels forlag.

Johansson, Karl G. 2005. 'Översättning och originalspråkstekst i handskriftstraderingens våld: *Merlínusspá* och *Vǫluspá* i Hauksbók'. In *Neue Ansätzte in der Mittelalterphilologie. Nye veier i middelalderfilologien: Akten der skandinavistischen Arbeitstagung in Münster vom 24. bis 26. Oktober 2002*, 97–113. Ed. S. Kramarz-Bein. Texte und Untersuchungen zur Germanistik und Skandinavistik 55. Frankfurt am Main: Peter Lang.

Jón lærði Guðmundsson. 1916. *Fjölmóður. Ævidrápa*. Ed. Páll Eggert Ólason. Safn til sögu Íslands og ísl. bókmennta V: 3. Reykjavík: Hið íslenska bókmenntafélag.

Jón Guðnason. 1961. *Dalamenn: Æviskrár 1703–1961* II. Reykjavík: Gefið út á kostnað Höfundar.

Jón Helgason. 1926. *Jón Ólafsson frá Grunnavík*. Safn Fræðafjelagsins um Ísland og Íslendinga 5. Kaupmannahöfn: Gefið út af hinu íslenzka Fræðafélagi í Kaupmannahöfn.

Jón Helgason. 1948. 'Bókasafn Brynjólfs biskups'. *Landsbókasafn Íslands: Árbók 1946–1947*, 115–147.

Jón Helgason. 1962–1981. *Íslensk fornkvæði: Islandske folkeviser* I–VIII. Editiones Arnamagnæanæ B 10–17. København: Ejnar Munksgaard.

Jón Helgason. 1970. 'Sevels islandske håndskrifter'. *Opuscula* 4 (*Bibliotheca Arnamagnæana* 31), 108–119. Hafniæ: Munksgaard.

Jón Helgason. 1985. 'Bækur og handrit á tveimur húnvetnskum höfuðbólum á 18du öld'. *Landsbókasafn Íslands: Árbók 1983*, 5–46.

Jón Helgason. [not yet published]. *Katalog over islandske håndskrifter i The British Library*.

Jón Jóhannesson (ed.). 1956. *Íslendingabók Ara fróða. AM. 113a and 113b, fol.* Reykjavík: University of Iceland.

Jón Ólafsson úr Grunnavík. 1950. 'Um þá lærðu Vídalína'. In *Merkir Íslendingar* IV 71–179. Ed. Þorkell Jóhannesson. Reykjavík: Bókfellsútgáfan.

Jónas Kristjánsson. 1967. *Skrá um íslenzk handrit í Svíþjóð.* Handritastofnun Íslands. [Unpublished]

Jónas Kristjánsson. 1987. 'Um Grógaldur og Fjölsvinnsmál'. In *Grímsævintýri sögð Grími M. Helgasyni sextugum 2. september 1987* II 13–15. Reykjavík: Stofnun Árna Magnússonar á Íslandi.

Jónas Kristjánsson (ed.). 2002. 'Hrafnagaldur Óðins — Forspjallsljóð: Fornkvæði reist úr ösku'. *Lesbók Morgunblaðsins* 27/4 2002, 4–6.

Jorgensen, Peter. 1977. '*Hafgeirs saga Flateyings*: An Eighteenth-Century Forgery'. *Journal of English and Germanic Philology* LXXVI 155–164.

Kristján Árnason. 2002. '"Hljóðdvöl" í Hrafnagaldri Óðins'. *Lesbók Morgunblaðsins* 25/5 2002, 11.

Kålund, Kristian. 1900. *Katalog over de oldnorsk-islandske Håndskrifter i Det Store Kongelige Bibliotek.* København: Gyldendal.

Lassen, Annette. 2006. 'Hrafnagaldur Óðins / Forspjallsljóð: Et antikvarisk digt?' In *The Fantastic in Old Norse/Icelandic Literature. Sagas and the British Isles. Preprint Papers of the 13th International Saga Conference. Durham and York, 6th–12th August, 2006,* I 551–560. Ed. John McKinnell, David Ashurst and Donata Kick. Durham.

Loth, Agnete. 1960. 'Om nogle af Ásgeir Jónssons håndskrifter'. *Opuscula* 1 (*Bibliotheca Arnamagnæana* 20) 207–212. Hafniæ: Munksgaard.

LP = Sveinbjörn Egilsson. 1931. *Lexicon Poeticum antiquæ linguæ septentrionalis. Ordbog over det norsk-islandske skjaldesprog.* Rev. Finnur Jónsson. København: Det Kongelige Nordiske Oldskrift-Selskab.

Már Jónsson. 1998. 'Þórður biskup Þorláksson og söfnun íslenskra handrita á síðari hluta 17. aldar'. In *Frumkvöðull vísinda og mennta: Þórður Þorláksson biskup í Skálholti,* 179–196. Ed. Jón Pálsson. Reykjavík: Háskólaútgáfan.

Meissner, Rudolf. 1921. *Die Kenningar der Skalden.* Bonn und Leipzig: Kurt Schroeder.

Morawski, Joseph. 1925. *Proverbes français antérieurs au XVe siècle.* Paris: É. Champion.

Noreen, Adolf. 1923. *Altisländische und Altnorwegische Grammatik.* Halle: Max Niemeyer.

Norrœn fornkvæði. 1867. Ed. Sophus Bugge. Christiania: Malling.

Ólafur Halldórsson. 1967. *Skrá yfir íslenzk og norsk handrit í Edinborg* I–III. Stofnun Árna Magnússonar á Íslandi. [Unpublished]

ONP = Ordbog over det norrøne prosasprog I– . 1995– . København: Den Arnamagnæanske Kommission.

ONP word list: http://dataonp.hum.ku.dk/index.html

Orðabók Háskólans: http://www.lexis.hi.is/indexny.html

Orkneyinga saga. Ed. Finnbogi Guðmundsson. In *ÍF* XXXIV 3–300.

Páll Eggert Ólason. 1918– . *Skrá um handritasöfn Landsbókasafnsins* I–V. Reykjavík: Landsbókasafn Íslands.

Parkin, John. 2006. *La Renaissance et la nuit* (review). *French Studies* LX 379–380.

Philosophia Patrum = Wegeler, J. 1877. *Philosophia Patrum in lateinischen Versen und ihre Übersetzungen*. Koblenz.

Porter, Pamela. 2006. 'Preserving the Past: England, Iceland and the Movement of Manuscripts'. *Care and Conservation of Manuscripts* IX 173–190.

Rímnatal I–II. 1966. Compiled by Finnur Sigmundsson. Reykjavík: Rímnafélagið.

Ritaukaskrá Landsbókasafnsins 1925. 1926. Reykjavík: Landsbókasafn Íslands.

Sandvig, B. C. (trans.). 1783–1785. *Forsøg til en Oversættelse af Sæmunds Edda* I–II. Kiøbenhavn.

Scheving, Hallgrímur (ed.). 1837. *Hrafnagaldur Óðins / Forspiallslióþ. Bodsrit Bessastada skóla 1837*. Videyjar klaustri.

Scheving, Hallgrímur. 1843. 'Islendskir málshættir safnadir, úrvaldir og í stafrófsrød færdir'. *Bodsrit Bessastadaskóla 1843*. Videyjar klaustri.

Schück, Henrik. 1933. *Kgl. Vitterhets historie och Antikvitets Akademien dess förhistoria och historia* III. Stockholm.

Seelow, Hubert. 1977. 'Ásgeir Jónsson und seine "Membranartige" Frakturschrift'. In *Sjötíu ritgerðir helgaðar Jakobi Benediktssyni 20. júlí 1977*, II 658–664. Ed. Jónas Kristjánsson and Einar G. Pétursson. Rit 12 . Reykjavík: Stofnun Árna Magnússonar á Íslandi.

Sievers, Eduard. 1893. *Altgermanische Metrik*. Halle: Max Niemeyer. Sammlung Kurzer Grammatiken germanischer Dialekte. Ergänzungsreihe 2.

SnE 1848–1887 = *Edda Snorra Sturlusonar* I–III. Ed. Jón Sigurðsson, Finnur Jónsson and Sveinbjörn Egilsson. Hafniæ: Sumptibus Legati Arnamagnæani.

SnE 1931 = *Edda Snorra Sturlusonar*. Ed. Finnur Jónsson. København.

SnE I–II = *Snorri Sturluson: Edda* [I]. *Prologue and Gylfaginning*. Second edition. Ed. Anthony Faulkes. 2005. London: Viking Society for Northern Research. [II]. *Skáldskaparmál. Introduction, Text and*

Notes. Ed. Anthony Faulkes. 1998. London: Viking Society for Northern Research.

Stefán Karlsson (ed.). 1983. *Guðmundar sögur biskups* I. *Ævi Guðmundar biskups*. *Guðmundar saga* A. Editiones Arnamagnæanæ B 6. København: C. A. Reitzel.

Stefán Karlsson. 2000. 'Tungan'. In *Stafkrókar: Ritgerðir eftir Stefán Karlsson gefnar út í tilefni af sjötugsafmæli hans*. Ed. Guðvarður Már Gunnlaugsson. Rit 49, 19–75. Reykjavík: Stofnun Árna Magnússonar á Íslandi. Translated by Rory McTurk as *The Icelandic Language*. 2004. London: Viking Society for Northern Research.

Sveinbjörn Rafnsson. 1999. 'Merlínusspá og Vǫluspá í sögulegu samhengi'. *Skírnir* CLXXIII 377–419.

Sørensen, John Kousgård (ed.). 1980. *Danmarks gamle ordsprog* 6: *Samlinger fra det 17. århundrede*. København: C. A. Reitzel.

Sørensen, John Kousgård (ed.). 1988. *Danmarks gamle ordsprog* 7/2: *Danske ordsproge* I, *Kiøbenhafn 1688 / Peder Syv*. København: C. A. Reitzel.

Verri, Giovanni. 2007. 'Nokkur óþekkt handrit *Hrafnagaldurs Óðins / Forspjallsljóðs*'. Ritgerð til BA-prófs í íslensku fyrir erlenda stúdenta. Hugvísindadeild Háskóla Íslands. Reykjavík. [Unpublished]

Veturliði Óskarsson. 2003. *Middelnedertyske låneord i islandsk diplomsprog frem til år 1500*. Bibliotheca Arnamagnæana XLIII. København: C. A. Reitzel.

Walther, Hans. 1963–1969. *Lateinische Sprichwörter und Sentenzen des Mittelalters in alphabetischer Anordnung* I–VI. Göttingen: Vandenhoeck und Ruprecht.

Ward, H. L. D. 1893. *Catalogue of Romances in the Department of Manuscripts in the British Museum* II. London: Printed by order of the trustees.

Weggewohnts Lied (Vegtams kvida), Der Odins Raben Orakelsang (Hrafna galdr Odins) und Der Seherin Voraussicht (Völuspâ). 1875. Ed. Friedrich Wilh. Bergmann. Strassburg: Trübner.

Þorsteinn Þorsteinsson. 1935. *Magnús Ketilsson sýslumaður*. Reykjavík: Félagsprentsmiðjan.

INDEX OF MANUSCRIPTS

Add. 4877 (4877): 28, 39, 46–48, 64
Add. 11165 (11165): 28, 39, 50, 64
Add. 11245: 37
Add. 29537: 45
Adv. 21.4.7 (21.4.7): 28, 39, 45–50, 64
Adv. 21.5.2 (21.5.2): 28, 50, 54–55, 57–60, 64
Adv. 21.6.7 (21.6.7): 28, 54, 61–64, 70, 77
AM 212 fol.: 14
AM 242 fol. (Codex Wormianus): 26
AM 424 fol.: 8: 21n, 22, 26–27, 76
AM 433 fol.: 17
AM 544 4to (Hauksbók): 43, 95–96
AM 551 d β 4to: 14
AM 582 4to: 77
AM 748 I a 4to: 43
AM 916 4to: 48n
AM 927 4to: 65
AM 254 8vo: 14
Bjarni Halldórsson's manuscript (B): 40, 52, 77
Codex Langebekianus: 43n, 44–45
Egerton 642: 57
Egerton 643 (643; Codex Thorlacianus): 28, 50, 55–57, 59, 64
Eyjólfur Jónsson's manuscript: 39–40, 42–43, 46, 49, 77
GKS 2365 4to (Codex Regius of the eddic poems): 7, 11–15, 21, 26, 29–30, 36, 40, 43, 45–46, 48–50, 54, 56–61, 66, 68, 70–71, 80, 97, 102
Geir Vídalín's manuscript: 8–9, 78
Gunnar Pálsson's manuscript: 22, 77, 79
Harl. 3362: 20
ÍBR 36 4to (36): 27, 71–73
ÍBR 24 8vo (24): 27, 71, 74–75
ÍBR 25 8vo: 74
ÍBR 26 8vo: 74
ÍBR 120 8vo: 17n
Jón Egilsson's manuscript: 39, 42–43, 46, 49, 77, 79
JS 273 4to a II 7: 17
JS 648 4to (648): 28, 50–51, 54–56, 59, 64
JS 391 8vo (391): 19
JS 470–519 8vo: 73
JS 494 8vo (494): 28, 71–74
KB Add 14 4to (14): 26–27, 76
Lbs 214 4to: 49, 58–59
Lbs 818 4to (818): 27, 61–64

Lbs 966 4to (966): 27, 38–39, 54, 63–65
Lbs 1199 4to (1199): 19
Lbs 1441 4to (E): 7, 14, 27, 29–30, 37, 64–71, 73, 81–94, 102
Lbs 1562 4to (B): 7, 12n, 13–14, 23, 27–28, 30, 35–39, 41, 43, 47, 49–51, 55–56, 59, 62–71, 80–94, 96
Lbs 1588 a 4to (1588 a): 27, 36, 40, 50–57, 59–60, 64, 77
  Lbs 1588 a I 4to (1588 a I): 27, 50–56, 64, 77
  Lbs 1588 a II 4to (1588 a II): 27, 50–57, 59–60, 64
Lbs 1689 4to (1689): 27, 50–51, 54–57, 59, 64
Lbs 2859 4to (2859): 27, 71, 75–76
Magnús Jónsson's manuscript: 61, 63, 77
Ms. germ. qu. 329 (329): 28, 50, 55, 58–60, 64
Ms. Icel. 47 (47; Codex Ericianus): 8–9, 28, 32, 39, 43–47, 64, 67, 76
NKS 1108 fol. (1108): 9, 27, 38–39, 48–51, 59, 64
NKS 1109 fol. (1109): 9, 27, 38–43, 46–47, 49–50, 52, 64, 77
NKS 1111 fol. (1111): 9, 27, 50, 54–55, 60, 64
NKS 1852 4to: 40
NKS 1866 4to (1866; Codex Luxdorphianus): 9, 27, 38–39, 42–50, 64, 79
NKS 1869 4to: 60
NKS 1870 4to (1870): 27, 31–32, 34, 44, 76, 79–80
NKS 1878 a 4to: 48n
Páll Hjálmarsson's manuscript: 77
Rostgaard 48 8to: 20n
Stockholm papp. fol. nr 34 (34): 8, 27, 30–34, 36, 76, 96–97
Stockholm papp. fol. nr 57 (C): 7, 9, 14, 27–30, 37, 64–71, 81–94
Stockholm papp. 4to nr 11 (11): 27, 33–34, 81, 88
Stockholm papp. 4to nr 46 (46): 8, 27, 33–34
Stockholm papp. 8vo nr 3: 29
Stockholm papp. 8vo nr 15 (A): 7–9, 12n, 13–14, 23, 27–31, 33–34, 36–37, 44, 62, 64–71, 79–94, 106
Stockholm papp. 8vo nr 18: 29
Thott 773 a fol. (773 a): 27, 39–43, 46–47, 49–50, 64
Thott 1491 4to (D): 7, 13–14, 27, 29–30, 37, 44, 64–71, 77, 81–94
Thott 1492 4to (1492): 27, 39–43, 46–47, 49–50, 64
UUB R 682 (682): 27, 32–34
UUB R 682 a (682 a): 27, 33–34
UUB R 684: 32
UUB R 691 (691): 27, 32, 34
ZCJ22 (22): 28, 39, 47–48, 64
Þórður Jónsson's manuscript: 58n, 66

INDEX OF NAMES

Adagia: 18–20
Aeneid: 24–25
Afguder heidingjanna: 63
Afzelius, Arvid August (1785–1871): 8, 10n
Ágrip af Postula-æfum: 73
Aldarháttur: 48
Álfrǫðull (alternative name for the sun): 94, 106
Alfǫðr (alternative name for Óðinn): 23, 82, 95
Alsviðr (alternative name for Óðinn?): 83, 97
Alsvinnsmál: 105
Alvíssmál: 29, 32–33, 42, 44, 61, 63, 72, 74, 98, 105–106
Antikvitetskollegiet: 29, 31, 79
Arnamagnæan Commission, The: 17n, 40n, 58, 76
Árni Böðvarsson (1713–1776): 49, 51
Árni Magnússon, Professor (1663–1730): 11–15, 58, 76–77, 79
Árni Þorkelsson (1730–1801): 51
Árni Þorsteinsson (1754–1829): 16
Arons saga: 14
Ásbjarnarkviða: 62
Ásgeir Jónsson (c. 1657–1707): 12n, 21, 28, 35–37, 64
Atlakviða: 36, 63, 72
Atlamál in grœnlenzku: 35–36, 63, 72
Baldr (a god): 98, 104
Baldrs draumar: 10n, 11n, 21n, 23–24, 26, 29, 32, 35–36, 38, 40, 43–46, 48–50, 54, 56–58, 60–61, 63, 68, 72–73, 76, 80, 104, 106
Banks, Joseph (1743–1820): 46, 78
Bárðar saga Snæfellsáss: 18
Bartholin (the Elder), Thomas (1616–1680): 29
Bartholin, (the Younger), Thomas (1659–1690): 12n, 79
Bergbúa þáttr: 68, 72
Bifrǫst (the gods' bridge to heaven): 25, 86, 99, 106
Bjarkamál: 62, 72
Bjarnasona kvæði: 64
Bjarni Halldórsson (1703–1773): 40, 52, 77
Björn Jónsson of Skarðsá (1574–1655): 66
Björn M. Ólsen, Professor (1850–1919): 38
Bogi Benediktsson of Staðarfell (1771–1849): 52
Borch, Ole, Professor (1626–1690): 29
Bóthildar kvæði: 64
Bowring, John (1792–1872): 45n
Bragi (a god): 7, 23n, 86, 89, 98–99, 102
Breiðfjörð, Sigurður (1798–1846): 51
Brísingamen: 74
Brot af Sigurðarkviðu: 31, 36
Brynjólfur Brynjólfsson: 38
Brynjólfur Sveinsson, Bishop (1605–1675): 11–15, 19–22, 79
Bugge, Sophus, Professor (1833–1907): 9–12, 14, 17n, 30–31, 34, 38, 41, 43n, 44–45, 49, 61, 65, 71, 75–76, 80n, 81, 102–104, 106
Bǫlverkr (alternative name for Óðinn): 91, 103
Ceciliu kvæði: 64
Clarke, Adam (d. 1832): 56
Constable, Archibald (1774–1827): 56
Copenhagen: 10, 15, 17n, 20, 23, 27, 37, 44, 48n, 53, 58, 65, 76, 79–80, 95
Dáinn (a dwarf): 83, 88, 96, 101
Dellingr (father of Day): 93, 98, 105
Dráp Niflunga: 72
Duhre, Gabriel: 33–34
Dvalinn (a dwarf): 93, 105
Ebba kvæði: 64
Edda, see Snorri's *Edda*
Eggert Ólafsson (1726–1768): 45, 52, 58–60
Egill Skallagrímsson (10th century): 46, 48, 58, 62–63, 68
Einar Bjarnason from Starrastaðir (1782–1856): 72

Einar Hálfdanarson, Síra (1695–1753): 53
Eiríksmál: 62
Eiríkur Hallsson at Höfði, Síra (1614–1698): 20–21
Elenar ljóð: 64
Élivágar (primeval waters or rivers): 88, 101
Engilbert Jónsson, Síra (1747–1820): 52
Erasmus of Rotterdam (1466–1536): 18–20
Erlendur Hjálmarsson (1750–1835): 52
Eyjólfur Jónsson at Vellir, Síra (1670–1745): 17n, 39–43, 46, 49, 77, 79
Eyvindr Finsson skáldaspillir (d. c. 990): 62
Fáfnismál: 47, 63, 72, 99, 105
Fenrir (a wolf): 93, 103–104
Finnur Jónsson, Bishop (1704–1789): 68
Finnur Magnússon, Professor (1781–1847): 10, 13n, 45, 50, 56–57, 72, 78
Fjölsvinnsmál: 14, 29, 35–36, 38–40, 43–44, 46, 48–50, 54, 56–58, 60–61, 63, 66, 68, 72, 75–76, 100
Fornjótr (a giant): 90, 103
Frá dauða Sinfjǫtla: 63, 72–73
Frigg (a goddess): 14, 93, 104–105
Fuglagáta: 63
Fundinn Noregr: 74
Gamla jólaskrá: 63
Gauta kvæði: 64
Geir Vídalín, see Vídalín, Geir
Ginnungi/Ginnungr (a mythological figure or place): 83, 97
Gísli Brynjúlfsson (1827–1888): 12
Gísli Jónsson Steinhólm (1804–1860): 38
Gísli Konráðsson (1787–1877): 51
Gísli Þorláksson, Bishop (1631–1684): 21
Gizurr gullbrárskáld (d. c. 1030): 62
Gjallarhorn (Heimdallr's horn): 86, 89, 94, 97, 99, 102, 106
Gjǫll (name of a river): 86, 99, 106
Glælognskviða: 62
Gráfeldar drápa: 62
Grettis saga: 72
Grímnir (alternative name for Óðinn): 30, 89, 102
Grímnismál: 10n, 25n, 26, 29, 32, 35, 61, 63, 72, 74, 95–106
Grímur Thorkelín, see Thorkelín, Grímur
Grípisspá: 63, 72
Grottasǫngr: 14, 26, 29, 31, 35–36, 38, 40, 43–44, 46, 48–50, 54, 56–58, 60, 62–63, 65–66, 68, 72, 75
Gróugaldur: 11, 14, 29, 35, 38–40, 43–44, 46, 49–50, 54, 56–58, 60, 62–63, 66, 68, 72–73, 75–76
Grundtvig, N. F. S. (1783–1872): 10n
Grüner, Johan Diderik (1661–1712): 29, 32
Grænlandsannáll: 79n
Guðbrandur Vigfússon (1827–1889): 17n, 47–48
Guðbrandur Þorláksson, Bishop (c. 1541–1627): 97
Guðmundar sǫgur biskups: 14
Guðmundur Andrésson (d. 1654): 31
Guðmundur Einarsson (1823–1865): 72
Guðmundur Gísli Sigurðsson, Síra (1834–1892): 74
Guðmundur Ísfold, see Ísfold, Guðmundur
Guðmundur Magnússon (1741–1798): 8–9, 11n, 13n, 16, 18, 20–21, 23, 27, 31, 44, 76, 78
Guðmundur Ólafsson (c. 1652–1695): 12n, 21, 28–29, 31, 33, 36, 79
Guðrún Jónsdóttir: 38
Guðrúnarkviða I: 31, 36, 63, 72, 74
Guðrúnarkviða II: 36, 63, 72
Guðrúnarhvǫt: 36, 63, 72
Gullkársljóð: 56, 59
Gunnar Pálsson (1714–1791): 8–9, 10n, 16–17, 21n, 22, 26–27, 39, 76–77, 79, 80n
Gunnarsslagur: 16–17, 21, 72–74
Gunnlaugs saga: 76
Guttormr sindri (10th century): 62
Guttormur Pálsson, Síra (1775–1860): 16
Hafgeirs saga Flateyings: 17
Hákonar saga Hákonarsonar: 14, 64
Hákonarmál: 58, 62, 68, 72

Index of Names

Háleygjatal: 25, 105
Hálfdan Einarsson, Principal (1732–1785): 17n
Halldór Hjálmarsson, Vice–Principal (1745–1805): 51–53, 77
Hallgrímur Pétursson, Síra (1614–1674): 51
Hallgrímur Scheving, see Scheving, Hallgrímur
Hallmundar vísur/Hallmundar ljóð: 14, 62, 64
Hamðismál: 23, 35–36, 40, 43, 45, 48, 54, 56–59, 61, 63, 66, 68, 72, 75
Hangatýr (alternative name for Óðinn): 25, 90, 103
Hárbarðsljóð: 29, 32–33, 51, 61, 63, 72, 74, 76
Háttalykill Lopts ins ríka: 72
Háttalykill Þorláks Guðbrandssonar Vídalíns: 48
Hávamál: 15, 22, 25n, 29, 32–33, 35–36, 38, 50, 52, 56, 61, 63, 65–66, 72–74, 76, 96, 103, 105
Loddfáfnismál: 52, 56, 96
Rúnatal: 32
Heiðreks gátur: 11, 35–36, 40, 43, 46, 48–50, 60, 62–63, 68, 72, 80
Heimdallr (a god): 7, 23, 86, 89, 91, 94, 99, 101–103, 106
Heimskringla: 26, 58, 74, 97, 103, 105
Ynglinga saga: 26, 97, 103, 105
Heinsius, Daniel (1580–1655): 18
Hel (world of the dead): 87, 98–100; daughter of Loki 100, 106
Helgakviða Hjǫrvarðssonar: 63, 72, 74
Helgakviða Hundingsbana I: 63, 72, 74
Helgakviða Hundingsbana II: 72, 74
Helgi Hundingsbani (legendary hero): 57
Helgi Ólafsson (c. 1646–1707): 31, 36, 44, 52–53, 64, 76, 96–97
Hellisvísur: 72
Helreið Brynhildar: 36, 63, 71
Henderson, Ebenezer (1784–1858): 61
Herjan (alternative name for Óðinn): 89, 97, 99
Hersleb, Peder, Bishop (1689–1757): 42, 79

Himinbjǫrg (place at the edge of heaven): 94, 106
Hjaltalín, Jón A., Síra (1840–1908): 75–76
Hliðskjálf (Óðinn's lookout place): 86, 100
Hlýrnir (the sixth of the mythological heavens): 87, 100
Hnikarr (alternative name for Óðinn): 91, 104
Hólar, Hjaltadalur: 21, 39, 53, 77, 79, 98
Hólmfríður Vídalín, see Vídalin, Hólmfríður
Hornklofavísur: 58
Hrímfaxi (Night's horse): 93, 104–105
Hroptr (alternative name for Óðinn): 54, 93, 104
Hugsvinnsmál: 72–74
Hvad Galldur kallast: 63
Hvǫrnenn lita skal hier-lendst: 63
Hymiskviða: 29, 61, 63, 72, 74, 76, 101
Hyndluljóð: 14, 26, 29, 35–36, 38, 40, 43–44, 46, 48–50, 53–54, 56–61, 63, 66, 68, 72, 80, 96, 99, 106
Hǫfuðlausn: 45–46, 52, 62–63, 68, 72
Iðunn (a goddess): 7, 24, 26, 84, 97–102
Iliad: 24
Ísfiord, Þorlákur Magnússon (c. 1748–1781): 17n
Ísfold, Guðmundur (1732–1782): 68
Íslendingabók: 14
Ívaldr (a dwarf): 82, 98
Íviðja (a trollwife): 81, 95
Jóhann Jónsson: 74
Jóhanna Soffía Bogadóttir (1823–1855): 62
Jómsvíkingadrápa: 48, 59
Jón A. Hjaltalín, see Hjaltalín, Jón A.
Jón Bjarnason of Rafnseyri, Síra (1721–1785): 38
Jón Eggertsson (1800–1880): 47
Jón Egilsson, Síra, Vice-principal (1714–1784): 39, 42–43, 46, 49, 77, 79
Jón Egilsson at Stóra-Vatnshorn (1724–1807): 61, 77
Jón Eiríksson (1728–1787): 8–9, 32, 44, 67, 76

Jón Erlendsson of Villingaholt, Síra (d. 1672): 14–15
Jón Gíslason Steinhólm (1756–1828): 38
Jón (lærði) Guðmundsson (1574–1658): 22, 79n
Jón Halldórsson, Síra (1665–1736): 11, 12n, 49, 58, 77
Jón Jónsson at Flugumýri and Hjaltastaðir, Síra (1725–1799): 66
Jón Jónsson langur (1779–1828): 73
Jón Jónsson skon (d. 1695): 51
Jón Níelsson of Grænanesi (1800–1842): 74
Jón Ólafsson at Eyri (1729–1778): 39, 77
Jón Ólafsson of Grímsstaðir (c. 1691 to c. 1765): 62
Jón Ólafsson of Grunnavík (1705–1779): 14–15, 17, 37, 40, 72
Jón Sigurðsson (1811–1879): 65
Jón Sigurðsson Dalaskáld (c. 1685–1720): 51
Jónas Jónsson: 61
Jórunn (alternative name for Iðunn?): 89, 102
Julius, Nikolaus Heinrich (1783–1862): 59
Kolbeinn Bjarnason (1752–1833): 62
Krákumál: 56, 59, 68, 72
Kristín Skúladóttir (1809–1880): 47
Kristínar kvæði: 64
Kristján Magnussen (1801–1871): 47–48
Krosskvæði: 51
Laufás Edda: 36, 52
Lesrím Ó. Hjaltalíns: 73
Lexicon Islandicum: 31
Lítið ágrip um afguðina og gyðjurnar: 62
Lokasenna: 24, 25n, 29, 32–33, 35, 61, 63, 72–74, 76, 98–99, 103–104
Loki (a god): 7, 86, 89, 91, 93, 98–100, 102–105
Loptr (alternative name for Loki): 34, 86, 99
Luxdorph, Bolle Christensen (1643–1698): 29
Luxdorph, Bolle Willum (1716–1788): 39–40, 42–43, 78–79
Madden, Frederic (1801–1873): 50, 57
Magnús (digri) Jónsson of Vigur (1637–1702): 40, 61, 63, 77
Magnús (prúði) Jónsson (1525–1591): 19
Magnús Ketilsson (1732–1803): 47–48
Mannheimr (the world of men): 41, 43, 93, 105
Maríuvísur: 51
Markús Jónsson, Síra: 60
Marteins kviða: 64
Merlínusspá: 56, 58, 72
Metamorphoses: 24
Michaelis Apostolius: 18–20
Miðgarðr (rampart made by the gods): 15n, 88, 101
Mímir (mythological figure): 37, 41, 49, 84, 91, 97–98, 102
Munch, P. A., Professor (1810–1863): 8–11, 74
Møllmann, Bernhard, Professor (1702–1778): 17n, 40n
Nál (mother of Loki): 25, 89, 102
Niflheimr, Niflhel (world of mist or darkness): 25, 34, 94, 98, 106
Njóla (alternative name for night): 42, 48, 94, 106
Nockrar Málsgreiner um það hvadan Böken Edda hefir sitt nafn: 63
Nomenclaturæ vocum Grammaticarum Eddu authoris: 52
Nora eða Njörva jötuns kviða: 72
Noregs konungatal: 62
Nyerup, Rasmus, Professor (1759–1829): 59
Nǫrvi (father of Nótt): 85, 98
Oddi, Rangárvellir: 42, 45, 61, 68, 74
Oddrúnar grátr: 36, 63, 72
Óðhrærir (a mythological figure): 72, 82, 96
Óðinn (a god): 7, 21–24, 26, 38, 53, 86, 89–90, 92–93, 95–104
Ólafur Jónsson, Síra (1637–1688): 12–13, 21, 79
Ólafur Jónsson of Purkey: 38
Ólafur Sveinsson (1762–1845): 62
Ólufar kvæði: 64

Index of Names

Ómi (alternative name for Óðinn): 30, 92, 104
Páll Andrésson: 52
Páll Hjálmarsson, Síra (1752–1830): 52, 77
Páll (stúdent) Pálsson (1806–1877): 62, 73
Páll Sveinsson (1704–1784): 14, 44, 65–67, 77
Páll Vídalín, see Vídalín, Páll
Powell, Frederick York (1850–1904): 47
Ragnarǫk: 23–24, 80, 102–104, 106
Rakni (a sea-king): 104
Rask, Rasmus Kr., Professor (1787–1832): 8–9, 10n, 30–31, 33, 71, 74, 81, 100–104
Reginsmál: 72, 100
Resen, Peder Hansen, Professor (1625–1688): 15, 31, 68
Rígsþula: 26, 45–46, 54, 57, 68, 72
Rímur af hvarfi og drukknan árið 1768 Eggerts skálds Ólafssonar: 51
Rindr (a giantess): 93, 104
Rosenblad, Bernhard (1796–1855): 44
Rúnadeilur: 74
Rǫgnir (alternative name for Óðinn): 86, 100
Sandvig, Bertel Christian (1752–1786): 16n
Scheving, Hallgrímur (1781–1861): 8, 10, 18, 22, 24, 71, 73–74, 81, 95, 99, 101–104, 106
Scheving, Hallgrímur (b. 1846): 95
Scheving, Stefán (1766–1844): 95
Scheving, Vigfús Hansson (1735–1817): 52
Scheving, Vigfús Jónsson (1749–1834): 53n
Scheving, Þórunn Stefánsdóttir (1793–1881): 95
Scott, Walter (1771–1832): 56
Sevel, Frederik Christian (1723–1778): 49
Sigrdrífumál: 63, 66, 72, 74, 97, 103
Sigurðarkviða in skamma: 36, 63, 72
Sigurður Breiðfjörð, see Breiðfjörð, Sigurður
Sigurður Eiríksson, Síra (1706–1768): 16
Sigurður (skáldi) Jónsson (18th century): 51
Sigurður Vigfússon (1828–1892): 47
Siön Sira Jons Eyölfssonar: 63
Skafti Skaftason, Síra (1761–1804): 16
Skírnismál: 29, 32–33, 35, 61, 63, 72, 74, 100, 106
Skúli Magnussen: 47
Skúli Magnússon (1711–1794): 65
Skúli Thorlacius, see Thorlacius, Skúli
Skǫgul (valkyrie): 69, 91, 104
Snorri's *Edda*: 11n, 17n, 22–26, 30, 33, 40n, 41, 52–53, 57–58, 63, 95–106
   Gylfaginning: 22, 26, 96–106
   Skáldskaparmál: 42, 95–106
   Háttatal: 25n, 48
   See also *Laufás Edda*
Sólarljóð: 13–14, 23, 29, 32–33, 35–36, 38, 40, 43, 45–46, 48–52, 54, 58–61, 63, 68, 72–75, 79–80
Sonar harmur: 64
Sonatorrek: 43, 46, 56, 63, 68
Sotberg, Eric of (1724–1781): 33
Steele, Robert (1860–1944): 47
Stefán Scheving, see Scheving, Stefán
Stephens, George (1813–1895): 44–45
Stjúpmóður minning: 64
Stockholm: 12n, 26–27, 29, 31–32, 36, 44, 95
Suhm, Peter Friedrich (1728–1798): 32, 41, 43, 49, 61, 78–79
Sveinbjörn Egilsson, Principal (1791–1852): 95
Sveinbjörn Hallgrímsson, Síra (1815–1863): 95
Svipdagsmál I–II: 76
Systra kvæði: 64
Sæhrímnir (a boar): 15n, 91, 103–104
Sæmundr (fróði) Sigfússon (1056–1133): 9, 12, 14n, 23, 79–80
Sæmundur Hólm, Síra (1749–1821): 55–57
Taflkvæði: 64
Teikn til vedráttufars: 73

Third Grammatical Treatise: 25n
Thorkelín, Grímur, Professor (1752–1829): 57
Thorlacius, Børge, Professor and Rector (1775–1829): 16, 57
Thorlacius, Skúli (1741–1815): 12, 57
Thornton, Grace: 75
Thott, Otto, Count (1703–1785): 42, 44, 65, 78–79
Tillegg Nockurt heirande til Snorra Eddu, sem ecke er ad finna i þeim þricktu, ütdreiged af Skrife Biörns ä Skards ä: 66
Torfæus, Thormod (1636–1719): 63
Úlfrún (one of Heimdallr's mothers): 94, 106
Um Galldra Bækur: 63
Um oracula: 63
Upprune Galldra: 63
Urðr (mythological figure): 72, 82, 96, 98
Vafþrúðnismál: 10n, 29, 32–33, 35–36, 51, 61, 63, 72–74, 96, 98, 101, 104–106
Valagaldur Kráku: 56
Vallara kvæði: 64
Vellekla: 62
Vídalín, Geir, Bishop (1761–1823): 8–9, 78
Vídalín, Hólmfríður (1697–1736): 40
Vídalín, Páll, Principal (1667–1727): 22–23, 25, 36–37, 40, 52–53, 77, 79
Viðarr/Víðarr (alternative name for Óðinn): 90, 103
Viðrir (alternative name for Óðinn): 86, 99, 103
Vigfús Hansson Scheving, see Scheving, Vigfús Hansson
Vigfús Jónsson of Hítardalur, Síra (1706–1776): 49, 58
Vigfús Jónsson Scheving, see Scheving, Vigfús Jónsson
Vijsur Einars Skúla sonar um hinar nafnkunnugre Eijar vid Noreg: 52
Vingólf (alternative name for Gimlé): 25, 90, 103
Vísa trémanns í Sámseyju: 56, 62, 68
Vǫlundarkviða: 29, 32, 35, 40, 44, 53–54, 56–57, 63, 72–74

Vǫluspá: 10n, 11n, 13, 15, 22–26, 29, 31, 33, 35–36, 47, 55, 60–61, 63, 72–74, 80, 95–105
Worm, Ole, Professor (1588–1654): 29
Yggdrasill (the mythological worldtree): 84–85, 94–96, 98–99, 105–106
Yggjungr (alternative name for Óðinn): 54–55, 62–63, 67, 90, 103
Yggr (alternative name for Óðinn): 90, 99, 103
Ynglinga drápa: 74
Ynglingatal: 58, 72
Þórálfs drápa: 62
Þórarinn Jónsson, Síra (1755–1816): 51
Þorbjörg Magnúsdóttir (1667–1737): 40
Þorbjǫrn hornklofi: 22, 62
Þórður Jónsson of Staðarstaður, Síra (1672–1720): 58n, 66
Þórður Þorláksson, Bishop (1637–1697): 21
Þorfinnr munnr (d. c. 1030): 62
Þorgrímur Þorláksson: 52
Þorkels kviða: 64
Þorlákur Magnússon Ísfiord, see Ísfiord, Þorlákur Magnússon
Þorlákur Skúlason (1597–1656): 21
Þorleifur Jónsson of Skinnastaður, Síra (1845–1911): 56
Þormóðr Bersason Kolbrúnarskáld (d. c. 1030): 62
Þormóðr Trefilsson (11th century): 22
Þormóður Torfason, see Torfæus, Thormod
Þorn (a giant or a *svefnþorn*): 88, 101
Þorsteinn Eyjólfsson at Háeyri (c. 1645–1714): 11, 77
Þorsteinn Pétursson of Staðarbakki, Síra (1710–1785): 68
Þórunn Stefánsdóttir Scheving, see Scheving, Þórunn Stefánsdóttir
Þráinn (dwarf): 37, 41, 49, 75, 83, 96
Þrymskviða: 29, 32–33, 35, 40, 54, 56–59, 61, 63, 72–74, 101
Ögmundur Ögmundarson (c. 1681–1707): 37
Ǫrvar-Odds drápa: 62